About the Author:

Allen Wheelis was born in Louisiana in 1915 and spent his early years in San Antonio, Texas. He attended Louisiana State University and was graduated from the University of Texas, spending the following year doing graduate work in economics. He received his medical training at the College of Physicians and Surgeons, Columbia University, and served as Medical Officer in the Navy from 1943 to 1946. He was a Fellow of the Menninger Foundation School of Psychiatry, and a staff member of the Austen Riggs Center, Stockbridge, Massachusetts, and is a graduate of the New York Psychoanalytic Institute. Now in private practice in psychiatry and psychoanalysis in San Francisco, he is a staff member of the Mt. Zion Psychiatric Clinic and an instructor in the San Francisco Psychoanalytic Institute.

Dr. Wheelis has written for leading professional journals here and abroad and also for *The New Yorker. The Quest for Identity,* his first book, is arresting and brilliantly original. It is certain to take its place as one of the outstanding contributions to its field in recent years.

THE QUEST
FOR IDENTITY

Allen Wheelis

New York

THE QUEST
FOR IDENTITY

W · W · NORTON & COMPANY · INC·

for ILSE

CONTENTS

FOREWORD

This is an essay on man in mid-twentieth-century America. It is concerned with his changing character, with the loss of his old identity, and with his search for a new one. It is concerned, also, with psychoanalysis to which he turns with increasing frequency in this quest. The relevance of psychoanalysis to the treatment of neurosis is not in question here; but the relevance of psychoanalysis to the malaise of our times—to the quest for identity—is here subjected to critical examination.

The vantage point of this study is behind the couch. The generalizations derive, therefore, from observations of well-to-do urban people. There is, however, reason to believe that characterological changes which are due to occur widely appear first in this group; for it is here that the full range and variety of technological change is first experienced.

More directly this study derives from personal experience. No one is primarily interested in abstractions; one *becomes* interested, in the effort to achieve mastery of the unique and the immediate. The life that impacts on sense and feeling threatens at times to overwhelm us with complexity and conflict. At such times we have to take distance. We harness personal problems with generalities. When the outcome of this endeavor is a book, it is likely that the problems from which it arose were first the author's own, and only secondarily those he observed in others. By scholarly tradition, however, the disclosure of personal origin has no place in serious writing; the abstractions are presented in pure state. The reader applies them to his unique experience to see if they fit, if they add to his understanding of the bewildering elements of which his own life is composed; and he lines them up with other generalities which he has found useful, to see if they are compatible. But behind the abstractions lurks a shadow. Only by a sudden metaphor, a wry twist of phrase, does the reader sense that what he reads was wrought in conflict and sometimes anguish.

In this work the shadow is given substance. Interwoven with the abstractions is a thread of personal narrative—the events and faces out of the past of which these reflections are the current issue. The narrative does not establish the theory, nor is it meant to. It does not prove anything, but only illustrates. It illustrates what we were rather than what we are, what we are moving away from rather than what we are moving toward. It is an individual measure of social change. The figure which emerges is more characteristic of the nineteenth century than of the twentieth, and so, while native to this place, is a stranger to this time. The narrative sections thereby counterpoint, in substance as well as form, the theoretical sections which portray the emergent social character of today.

ACKNOWLEDGMENTS

In a slightly different form "Good-bye, Mama" was first published in *The New Yorker;* "The Vocational Hazards of Psychoanalysis" in *The International Journal of Psychoanalysis.* A small portion of Chapter I was taken from an article, "Will and Psychoanalysis," which was published in *The Journal of the American Psychoanalytic Association.*

The ideas of this work derive from many sources. Among these the author would acknowledge, particularly, his indebtedness to C. E. Ayres and to David Riesman.

It *is* glory—to have been tested, to have had our little quality and cast our little spell. . . . A second chance—*that's* the delusion. There never was to be but one. We work in the dark —we do what we can—we give what we have. Our doubt is our passion and our passion is our task. The rest is the madness of art.

HENRY JAMES

THE QUEST
FOR IDENTITY

I { THE EVOLUTION OF SOCIAL CHARACTER

THE OLD AND THE NEW

With increasing frequency in recent years a change in the character of the American people has been reported and described.[1] The change is within the lifetime of most persons of middle or advanced years, and the process of change is still underway. The social character [2] of ourselves and our children is unmistakably different from what we remember of the character of our grandparents.

Our grandparents had less trouble than we do in finding themselves. There were lost souls, to be sure, but no lost generation. More commonly then than now a young man followed his father, in character as in vocation, and often so naturally as to be unaware of having made a choice. Though the frontier was gone, there was still, for those who needed it, the open west. Sooner rather than later one found his calling; and, having found it, failure did not readily cause one to reconsider, but often was a goad to greater effort. The

17

goal was achievement, not adjustment; the young were taught to work, not to socialize. Popularity was not important, but strength of character was essential. Nobody worried about rigidity of character; it was supposed to be rigid. If it were flexible you couldn't count on it. Change of character was desirable only for the wicked.

Many of us still remember the bearded old men: the country doctor, the circuit rider, the blacksmith, the farmer. They were old when we were young, and they are dead now. We remember the high shoes, the heavy watch chain, the chewing tobacco, the shiny black suit on Sunday. The costume and make-up may still be seen, as they turn up in plays now and then. The character that went with them is disappearing, and soon even its memory will be lost.

Nowadays the sense of self is deficient. The questions of adolescence—"Who am I?" "Where am I going?" "What is the meaning of life?"—receive no final answers. Nor can they be laid aside. The uncertainty persists. The period of being uncommitted is longer, the choices with which it terminates more tentative. Personal identity does not become fixed, does not, therefore, provide an unchanging vantage point from which to view experience. Man is still the measure of all things, but it is no longer the inner man that measures; it is the other man. Specifically, it is the plurality of men, the group. And what the group provides is shifting patterns, what it measures is conformity. It does not provide the hard inner core by which the value of patterns and conformity is determined. The hard inner core has in our time become diffuse, elusive, often fluid. More than ever before one is aware of the identity he appears to have, and more than ever before is dissatisfied with it. It doesn't fit, it seems alien, as though the unique course of one's life had been determined by untoward accident. Commitments of all kinds—social, vocational, marital, moral—are made more tentatively. Long-term goals seem to become progressively less feasible.

Identity [3] is a coherent sense of self. It depends upon the awareness that one's endeavors and one's life make sense, that they are meaningful in the context in which life is lived. It depends also upon stable values, and upon the conviction that one's actions and values are harmoniously related. It is a sense of wholeness, of integration, of knowing what is right and what is wrong and of being able to choose.

During the past fifty years there has been a change in the experienced quality of life, with the result that identity is now harder to achieve and harder to maintain. The formerly dedicated Marxist who now is unsure of everything; the Christian who loses his faith; the workman who comes to feel that his work is piecemeal and meaningless; the scientist who decides that science is futile, that the fate of the world will be determined by power politics—such persons are of our time, and they suffer the loss or impairment of identity.

Identity can survive major conflict provided the supporting framework of life is stable, but not when that framework is lost. One cannot exert leverage except from a fixed point. Putting one's shoulder to the wheel presupposes a patch of solid ground to stand on. Many persons these days find no firm footing; and if everything is open to question, no question can be answered. The past half century has encompassed enormous gains in understanding and in mastery; but many of the old fixed points of reference have been lost, and have not been replaced.

The change in social character is often described as a decline of individualism; but individualism means many things, and not all of them have declined. Individualism means self-reliance, productive self-sufficiency, following one's chosen course despite social criticism, and bearing personally the risks of one's undertakings; and all of these are on the wane. Ours is an age of reliance on experts, of specialized production, of deference to public opinion, and of collective security. But individualism means, also, the awareness of individuality, and this has increased. For accompanying the other changes there has occurred an extension of awareness.

Modern man has become more perceptive of covert motivations, in both himself and others. Areas of experience formerly dissociated from consciousness have become commonplace knowledge. Passivity, anxiety, disguised hostility, masochism, latent homosexuality—these are not new with the present generation; what is new is the greater awareness of them. We deride the affectations which this heightened awareness so facilely serves—the "parlor psychiatry," the "curbstone interpretation"—but overlook the emergent fact of extended awareness of which the affectation is symptomatic. As man has lost his sense of identity he has, paradoxically, discovered more of those elements of his nature out of which identity may be formed, the raw materials with which to build. In losing the whole he has found some of the previously lost parts.

This extended awareness is both cause and effect of the loss of identity. It is a cause for the reason that identity is harder to achieve if renegade motivations have free access to consciousness. If one is able to deny with finality those lurking tendencies that run counter to the dominant trends of personality, then it is easier to know who one is and where one stands. This is of relevance in comparing the unsure man of today with his very sure grandfather. His sense of identity is less firm, but the elements he is called upon to integrate are more numerous and less homogeneous. The identity of his grandfather was like the log cabin of the frontier; it was small and dark, but it was put up with dispatch and was sturdy and snug. The grandson is fumbling as a builder, and keeps hankering to turn the whole job over to a professional architect; but it is to be noted that his job is harder. The materials with which he must work are more variegated. Their proper integration would achieve not a log cabin, but a more complicated and interesting structure, admitting more light and air and providing more room for living.

The extended awareness is also an effect of the loss of identity for the reason that, being unsure of who one is and where one stands, it behooves one to be more alert and perceptive. A firm sense of identity provides both a compass to determine one's course in life and ballast to keep one steady. So equipped and provisioned, one can safely ignore much of the buffeting. Without such protection more vigilance is needed; each vicissitude, inner and outer, must be defined and watched.

A change has occurred, also, in the dimensions of our existence. During this century, it is said, our lives have been both lengthened and narrowed. This makes reference to our longer life expectancy and to the increasing industrialization that is thought to diminish the meaning of life by the kind of work it imposes. The increased life span is indisputable, and doubtless much clerical and assembly line work is monotonous. Yet in a somewhat different sense the dimensional change is just the opposite of that proposed: our lives have been enriched cross-sectionally and diminished longitudinally.

In our time the range and variety of experience has been enormously extended. It is less integrated and less stable, but it is far wider in scope. Fifty years ago the great orchestras could be heard in only a few cities; now they are heard, by radio and recording, in every village across the continent. Comparable changes have occurred in the availability of all the arts. Better means of communication enable us to experience meanings that occur at great distances, better methods of travel to experience persons and areas heretofore inaccessible. Though these experiences are more easily had by the rich, they are to a notable degree available, also, to the assembly-line worker whose life is thought to be so impoverished. A war in Korea, a play on Broadway, a new philosophy in France—all are experienced more quickly and more widely than ever before.

Nor has the depth or meaningfulness of this experience been

diminished. When radios became common it was sometimes predicted that the musical taste of the nation would be depraved by the constant din of jazz. In fact, the relatively small amount of serious music that was broadcast along with the jazz developed the musical appreciation of millions. Serious music is now understood and valued by a far higher proportion of the people than would have been possible without the advent of radio. "Twenty years ago you couldn't sell Beethoven out of New York," reports a record salesman. "Today we sell Palestrina, Monteverdi, Gabrielli, and renaissance and baroque music in large quantities." [4] Parallel developments could be cited for countless other areas of experience. The gain in breadth of experience has generally been accompanied by a gain, also, in depth. Not only is the man of today constantly informed of a larger number of world events than was his grandfather; he understands them better. And within his own home he understands his children better. In all of these ways our lives have been cross-sectionally enriched.

But as our span of years has increased, our span of significant time has diminished. In some measure we have lost the sense of continuity with past and future. More and more quickly the past becomes outdated, and if we look back two or three generations the character and values of our forebears become as strange to us as their beards and high collars. Family portraits no longer hang in homes; there is no place for them in modern houses. And as we have lost touch with the past, so we have lost touch with the future. We know that we are in motion but do not know where we are going, and hence cannot predict the values of our children. Our grandfathers are likely to have dreamt of leaving as legacy a tract of land which would stay in the family and be maintained by their descendants; of building a house that would endure and be lived in after they were gone; of a profession that would become a tradition and be carried on by sons; of a name that would be wrought in iron over the carriage gate, the prestige of which would be shared and furthered by all who bore it. Seeing how these dreams have come to naught in us, we no longer try to direct or even to foresee the values of our descendants. We cannot now, with loving foresight, further their ends; for we do not know what ends they will pursue, nor where. We feel lucky if we can give our children an education. The founders of this country had a lively sense of the future, knew that posterity would vindicate their revolution, their moving west, their capitalism, their competition, their church. We—who have no idea of what posterity will honor—live more largely in the present.

Becker has pointed out that this is an age in which we cannot feel that we understand anything until we know its history.[5] As we become more aware of how things change, it becomes more important to know how they developed, how they got to be the way they are. But this does not mean that we feel more related to the past and future. It is rather the other way round: our feeling of estrangement in time and of the transience of the present prompts the historical approach. The historical approach is a symptom of our trouble. We are trying to recapture the sense of continuity, to find again the durable patterns of life—hoping we shall not lose altogether our connections with those who have lived before and those who will live after.

LEEVILLE

In 1898 Morris Hunt, then sixteen years old, left his father's farm and came to Leeville to go to school. He walked the eight miles, carrying his belongings on his back, and went to Mr. Dean's store, where he was to live. For several years thereafter he went to high school in the red-brick school, worked in the store, had his meals in Mr. Dean's house, and slept on a cot in the back of the store where the grain was kept.

He was a tall and slender boy, but strong, and he had a bony, angular face. His manner was marked by a quality of reserve and composure which strangers found disconcerting. Upon being addressed he would look steadily into the eyes of the speaker, listening with such still intentness as to suggest disbelief. And when the speaker had finished Morris would not reply immediately, but would continue in silence to gaze into the other's eyes, as if listening now to what had *not* been said. During these few moments he would seem to relate what he had heard to everything within his experience that had a bearing on it, and only then would he make reply. What he said in this deliberate way had an air of finality, and was rarely modified or retracted. He worked hard and became well-liked by Mr. Dean and by the people who entered the store to buy or who sat on the porch to talk.

Leeville was then a town of about two hundred people

situated in a forest of virgin pine in the northern part of Louisiana. The nearest towns of greater size were Ruston and Monroe, each about forty miles away—a long day's journey by horse and buggy over winding, red clay roads, dusty in dry weather and treacherously slick in wet. Approaching Leeville from Monroe, one's first view of the town would be from the crest of a low hill. Off to the right was Miss Ruby's place, an ancient house which was said to have been used as a storehouse for food by the Confederate Army. A little further, in a grove of trees, were the Methodist and Baptist churches, each painted white with a small belfry and steeple, and no more than a hundred yards apart. Beyond the churches was the new red-brick schoolhouse, which had four rooms. Passing over a creek and mounting a low incline, one came then to the center of town—two red stores, each a long narrow building extending back fifty yards from the street. One bore the sign, "O. H. Thurston, Merchant and Cotton Buyer"; the other, "J. H. Dean, General Merchandise." The space between these stores formed the village square where horses were tethered and wagons loaded. The square was completed by a livery stable on one side and by Doctor Thurston's residence on the other. On any summer afternoon one could see three or four men lounging on the benches in front of the stores. They wore straw hats tilted back on their heads, and their shirtsleeves were hitched up with colored garters. They looked on strangers in silence with a casual but curious stare.

At a distance of ten miles, through dense forests, ran the Ouachita River which was the principal avenue of contact with the outside world. Its waters rose in late winter and spring, became muddy and turbulent, and sometimes flooded the lowlands. But in summer and fall it was a clear stream, seventy-five yards wide, running a winding course between banks of variegated and luxuriant vegetation. There was a clearing and a pier, called the Alabama Landing because so many of the settlers had come there by water from Alabama. Birds called in the wilderness, and gar leaped from the water; and at night moonlight filtered through the trees, throwing mottled silver patterns on the matted pine needles. Somewhere nearby a still was operated, and here men sometimes came in groups at night to drink and play poker at the boathouse. Here fish fries were held and Sunday school picnics and family reunions. There was swimming and fishing and boating and the hunting of squirrel. Here girls were wooed and promises made and broken; and in the cool clear water Philip Cox was drowned that year, sucked down by a whirlpool.

Bayous opened their still mouths to the river's edge. They bore such names as *De l'Outre* and *De Siard*. In a small boat one could enter these stagnant channels and reach swamps of unearthly stillness. Hidden crags reached out and touched the bottom of the boat like huge dead fingers. Banks were vague and insubstantial, and over them an alligator might occasionally be seen to slither. The overhanging branches of tremendous, devitalized trees, parasitized beyond recognition by the sorrowful Spanish moss, formed twilight caverns. It was the province of copperheads and cottonmouth water moccasins and of the heron whose sudden scream would shatter the silence. After an initial flapping of wings, the angular white bird would glide low over the dead water, banking easily to avoid obstacles, wheeling and turning, rising and falling, skimming along over the still surface with only inches to spare, the white wings flickering through rotten branches, growing faint and inconstant, and disappearing finally in the gray silence.

On Saturday mornings the farmers would come to town to buy supplies; and, duties at home permitting, their wives and children would come too. The whole family would come riding into town on a wagon, the mother and father up front and the children in back. The square would be filled with teams of horses and the stores would be crowded. Though their business might be accomplished in a few minutes, they would spend the whole day. The man would buy flour, salt, and lard, and perhaps a bucket or an ax handle, or feed for the cattle. He would meet acquaintances and talk about crops, the lack of rain, the boll weevil, and the probable price of cotton in the fall. The wife would do more looking than buying. She would finger dresses and look at shoes and read the labels on canned goods; and in the end she would purchase only a bit of cotton goods and thread and buttons. But most of all she would talk. She would talk—with Mrs. Thurston, for example, who worked in the store on Saturdays—about the growth of their children and the health of their husbands. Going from place to place with this readiness to stop and chat, she would bring herself up to date on the town gossip, would find out that Mary Ellen was married, that Billy Jarvis was drinking as much as ever, and that the Reed boy had finally run away from home. As for the children, they were everywhere. They would explore smokehouses and wells, would clamber in and out of wagons, and would stand in the door of the blacksmith's shop and watch the shoeing of horses. The high point of their day would come when one of their parents would give them a penny for candy.

There was a lethargy on the square at noon of a summer's day—a haze, a drowsiness, a spell by which time seemed to stand still, a handful of moments in which hopes and desires all but forgotten stirred restlessly. Not so much as a breath of air would be stirring. The deep ruts made by wagon wheels during the last rain would long since have been baked to the hardness of stone, so to remain until the next siege of wet weather. The sun would glare from the red clay, and buildings viewed through rising heat waves would seem to quiver. Few people would be walking about at this hour, and those few would walk slowly, affected by a lethargy of heat. The stores were closed because the storekeepers would have gone home for lunch. Some of the families who had come to town to spend the day would have been asked to the homes of friends for dinner, but most of the people from the farms would sit on the porches of the stores and wait for the town's activity to resume. Some of them would have brought lunches—sandwiches of large white biscuits and pork sausage—and some would do without. Women would sit in the wagons nursing their babies, fanning away flies with straw hats. The Negroes would lie in the shade of the trees and sleep.

About four o'clock the farm people would get in their wagons and set out for home, feeling that a great day had come and gone. Not for a month would they have such pleasures or see such sights again. Their minds would turn to the work ahead—cattle to feed and care for, a fire to be built in the kitchen stove, and supper to cook. In the days to come there would be weeds to hoe from cotton, fences to build, fruit to can, clothes to sew, and wood to cut. And, in the loneliness of their pine wilderness, Leeville would appear in their memories as the center of the world, the place where something was always happening, where news traveled fast, and where all manner of wonderful things could be had by those with money to buy.

At the far side of the square was the Thurston residence— the largest house in town and the only one referred to as a "residence." It was a white house of thirteen rooms, one of which was built in the form of a tower. There were porches everywhere, all bounded by curving balustrades. The roof was high with many gables, each surmounted by a lightning rod with gold ball and spear tip. A white picket fence encircled the house, enclosing a large yard on all sides. In front of the house were six oak trees.

Beyond the house were a number of outhouses. Nearest to the kitchen door was the smokehouse, which had an earth floor and no windows, and smelled of pork and hickory smoke. Nearby was the privy and, only a few yards beyond, the well. Next came the chickenyard and chicken house, and beyond that an unpainted cabin where the Negro cook and her husband lived. The last and largest of the outhouses was the barn, which had stalls for three horses and room for two buggies. The barn opened onto a pasture at the far end of which was a shallow pond in a grove of pine trees.

The big house was built in 1885 when, except for Miss Ruby's place, Leeville had consisted of only a few isolated houses and the Thurston store. Oliver H. Thurston, who built it, was both the son and grandson of physicians. After completing the approximate equivalent of a high school education, he had apprenticed himself to his father, who practiced medicine in a small town in Alabama. Having acquired some practical experience, he then went to Nashville for his formal education—for "some courses in medicine" he called it. At the end of two winter semesters of six months each, he became a qualified practitioner. Five of his six brothers went to the same school. The sixth, it was said, became the best doctor of the lot without having bothered to take a medical degree. In those days the findings of Pasteur were regarded as a novelty; water was tested by holding it to the light to gauge the amount of suspended dirt; and major surgery was rarely attempted except in traumatic cases, and then was often fatal. The stock in trade of physicians was calomel, quinine, morphine, and purges.

The medical practice of one county of rural Alabama could not support eight doctors. "You couldn't turn around back there," it was said, "without stepping on a Doctor Thurston." For this and perhaps other reasons, Oliver moved west. In 1875, at the age of 27, he arrived by boat at the Alabama Landing and came to the place now known as Leeville. Though there was no town then, the region was being settled and had need of a physician. Deciding to stay, he built a small house, began to practice medicine, and married a farm girl named Molly Anderson. A year later, as the need for a store was as great as for a doctor, he journeyed to New Orleans, invested his capital in general merchandise, and returned to establish the first store within a radius of twenty miles. Previously the site of the future town had been uncertain, but with the advent of a store its location was determined. For this store became the center of social life, a place where people met, where news was spread, and where essential goods could be had, as well as medical services. The venture was successful. Soon Doctor Thurston had a sizable establishment which handled all types of goods from saddles to snuff, from bear traps to vinegar. In 1885, already the father of two sons, he was able to build the great house in which he still lived.

He built, also, an office for himself in the back of the store, and there saw patients. His office was always dusty and disordered; for he would allow no woman to come in to clean. The rolltop desk was never closed, and on it were piled circulars, pamphlets, correspondence, cascara tablets, obstetrical forceps, and a human skull. His medical practice took precedence over the business, and when a mesenger came to tell him that someone was sick he would leave the store and go. On almost any day in winter one could find two or three men sitting around the potbellied stove, chewing tobacco and talking. And it would never occur to Doctor Thurston to put them out and lock up just because he was going to be away for a while. If, during his absence, people came to buy, they would have to wait till he got back, or else take what they wanted and leave the money on the counter. For many years

he made his calls on horseback, carrying his drugs and instruments in saddlebags. But as the trails became wider and
log bridges were thrown up over creeks and gullies, he bought
a buggy.

He performed many important social functions in those
early days. He treated the ailments of the people, delivered
their children, officiated—when there was no churchman—at
their funerals, read essential printed matter for the illiterate,
sold them the necessary goods of life, pulled their teeth, spread
the news, dispensed drugs, bought their furs and cotton for
future sale in New Orleans, distributed mail when it arrived,
accepted letters for subsequent posting, doctored the cattle,
and gave westbound strangers directions as to the best way
to get to Texas, though "damned if I can see," he would say,
"why anybody'd want to go there." There were few people in
the region who did not owe him money, but he never took the
title to a man's land in payment for a defaulted debt. No one
was ever asked by him to sign a note, and never did he refuse goods from his store to those in need. For his medical
work he kept no books, and from the poor never sought nor
expected payment. Those few persons who could afford to
pay and yet did not, he called "trifling, damned, no-account
scoundrels," but in case of sickness he would visit the home
even of a scoundrel. He had six sons, two of whom died of
typhoid fever, and three daughters. The family lived well, but
Doctor Thurston accumulated no wealth.

In the 1880's land was being cleared, farms were expanding,
and settlers were coming in. There were quiltings and house-
raisings to help newcomers get established. Cowboys from

Texas came through in the spring with herds of horses; and the great event of the year was the auction of horses at that time. Occasionally the wild Cox boys would get drunk and ride through the town, shooting pistols and rifles.

Four times a year a steamboat would come up the Ouachita, bringing goods and settlers and taking out cotton and fur. Once each year Doctor Thurston would go to Monroe by buggy and on to New Orleans by train to buy goods; and he would time his trip so as to be able to accompany his purchases back on the boat. Twice Caroline, his oldest daughter, was allowed to accompany him, and these excursions remained in later years her most vivid childhood memories. She recalled her father's locking her in a hotel room to insure that she would get into no mischief, pacifying her with bananas, which she had never seen before. He had left early in the morning and not returned until night, and by then she was ill. With nothing else to do, she had spent the day eating the exotic yellow fruit. And she remembered the long trip home—up the Mississippi, into the turbulent Red, and then on the clear waters of the Ouachita, to arrive after eight days at the Alabama Landing. News of the boat's arrival would have spread through the country, and people would be there to meet them. There would be her envious younger brothers, her mother, and friends. Jim Turner might be there, hardly able to wait till the kissing was over before asking if the Doctor had got the rifle he wanted. And Molly would want to know if he had brought back apples and oranges, and someone else would be asking about buckshot or silk or spice. And all of these things he would have. When the goods were loaded on wagons, they would all get into buggies and ride back through the aromatic pine woods to the great house which was home.

Morris Hunt fell in love with Caroline Thurston when she was only thirteen, a black-haired girl with a face as soft and gentle as his was hard and angular. He decided then that eventually he would marry her, though it was not till some years later that he told her of this decision. When he finished school his wages were increased to twenty dollars monthly, in addition to food and lodging; and he saved this in preparation for his marriage. He did not like clerking in a store, and he did not like working for a boss. It was his intention to buy land and build a house and farm the land. When he was able to do this he would be able to get married.

In 1904 Doctor James, just out of medical school, came to Leeville to work with Doctor Thurston. Caroline's head was turned, and that summer she had little time for Morris. Doctor James lived in the Thurston home and had his meals with the family. In the evening he sat with Caroline in the porch swing, and on Sunday afternoons took her for buggy rides. Morris made no protest and displayed no curiosity, but he watched them carefully. He knew when they finished dinner; for he could hear the creak of the porch swing from Mr. Dean's store. Lying on his cot in the back of the store among the sacks of corn he could hear their laughter on the quiet summer nights. On Sundays he would watch them drive out of town in Doctor Thurston's buggy; when they had returned he would walk along the way they had gone and would learn where they had been and where they stopped and how long they stopped. When Doctor James sat down on the store front to pass the time of day with Mr. Dean, Morris would observe him closely. His hands were white and uncalloused; he always wore a coat and tie and hat; and his clothes were of a kind that could not be bought in Leeville. Morris noticed, also, how he talked and what he talked about, and learned something of life in a city from what Doctor James said of Nashville, its trains and trolley cars and big buildings and telephones. He listened also to what other people said about his rival. Doctor James had an easygoing manner and a ready flow of conversation. He seemed to be a good physician, and people liked him.

In September Doctor James left to enter private practice in New Orleans, where he had family connections. Caroline was despondent for a while, but soon recovered, and Morris might then have bought his land and got married, but by then he had made a different decision. "If it's a doctor you like," he said to Caroline, "it's a doctor I'll be." She protested against waiting four years, but he packed up his belongings and set out for Nashville. He was graduated from medical school in 1908, returned to Leeville, and began to practice medicine. He married Caroline and built a small house, and in the course of time they had three children—a girl, Helen; a boy who died of epidemic diarrhea; and another boy, Larry.

The town was changing. In 1903 sawmills had invaded the parish, and the great pine trees began to fall. A railroad was built to carry the logs, and the town blossomed for a while. An apothecary set up shop, a post office was established, and mail was delivered every day. A bank was built, Miss Ruby started a restaurant, two other stores handling general merchandise were opened, and Miss Ellis's big house on the hill by the depot was turned into a hotel. By 1915 there were thirty telephones in Leeville, and six automobiles, and the blacksmith sold gasoline and oil. The price of cotton fluctuated according to wars and the threat of wars. Small fortunes were made and lost. Planted with the same crop year after year, the land lost much of its fertility, which had not been great to start with. By 1917 the sawmills had cleared the parish and moved on to higher timber, leaving fields of stumps in their wake. But they held the land they had acquired, and the town ceased to grow.

The Thurston children were grown and scattered. The girls were married and, except for Caroline, had moved away. The boys found homes and wives and work in cities. They lived in Shreveport, Baton Rouge, and New Orleans, and worked in real estate, insurance, and banking.

In 1917 Morris joined the army as a medical officer. For several months Caroline and the children followed him, first to a camp in Augusta, then to one in Chattanooga. Then the moves became too frequent, and Morris sent them home to live with Caroline's parents until the war was over. In 1918 Morris had influenza in the epidemic and was a long time getting well. In 1919 he returned to Leeville and resumed his practice, but within a few months was sick with tuberculosis. Months dragged by and he couldn't get well. Finally he journeyed alone to San Antonio, where the dry, sunny climate was supposed to facilitate recovery, and for four months lay in a veterans' hospital. Nothing was done for him, for there was no treatment except rest. Rest, however, was nearly impossible for him. He was impatient to work, felt that his career was just beginning, and wanted to get on with it. To lie in bed day after day evoked a fury that was the opposite of rest.

It was all the more difficult because he could not feel at home in this strange land of black dirt and level ground. The mesquite that people called "trees" would have been called scrub brush in Leeville. If he had to rest, he decided that he would at least rest with his family. So he sent for Caroline to come and bring the children. With what was left of his savings he bought a house on the outskirts of San Antonio—a run-down house in a field of weeds and sunflowers. He had one porch of the house closed in with screens and glass, and this became his sickroom. He forced himself to lie in bed, but could not force himself to rest. He had his bed propped up so that he could see out, and was forever probing the countryside with telescope or binoculars. He watched the spiders and fed them flies; he had Larry put up an oatmeal box in a tree for the wrens; and when the sparrows would try to usurp this nest, Morris would shoot them from his sickbed with a .22 rifle, sometimes shooting through the screen wire. Here he lay and coughed, day after day, year after year, trying to get well.

THE CHANGE IN NEUROTIC PATTERNS

Doctor Thurston was a kind man and often was sympathetic with emotional disorders. He would prescribe tonics,

advise work, and would give generously of encouragement
and reassurance. When these measures did not help, however
—as often they did not—and when the patient became more
demanding, his patience would be short. Of a neurotic woman
he would say, "She's not sick, she's got hysterics." If her complaints were only in her mind then obviously they were not
real. "She just *thinks* she's sick." If he had made his call under
difficult conditions, he would be cross, would feel that his
time was being wasted. If she should prove hard to handle,
his sense of moral indignation would be indicated by his
readiness to shift the diagnosis from hysteria to malingering.
This was the attitude, also, of the patient's family and of society. She would receive little indulgence, but would be regarded with humor or derision. It was a disgrace, and if she
did not snap out of it the disgrace would deepen.

This intolerance amounted to a pressure against the emergence or admission of neurosis, and it had varying effects. It
forced the suppression of symptoms or the ability to live with
them and despite them and to keep going. It forced, also, some
curable neurotics into suicide, and it locked up and made
custodial cases of some who, in a different setting, might have
recovered.

This pressure has, in large measure, been replaced by tolerance. Now there is no difference in degree of reality between
mental and physical illness; one is as genuine as the other.
They differ in origin, development, and recovery, but are
alike in that in neither case is one expected simply to "snap
out of it." By this change in attitude neurosis has been admitted
into the realm of medicine, becoming entitled thereby to the

designation of illness, with all the rights and privileges pertaining thereunto. Among these are the right to professional attention and the privilege of delivering responsibility for the care and cure of one's illness into the hands of a physician. From the untoward consequences of this latter development psychiatrists are still trying, somewhat awkwardly, to extricate themselves.

The new orientation is regarded as a great social gain. Not only does it banish the old bigotry; it will also—we are assured—diminish the prevalence and severity of neurosis. For with the elimination of the stigma, the need for secrecy is gone. Since our culture does not enforce the suppression of neurosis, one is more free to acknowledge the difficulty and to seek help. And since psychiatric treatment is regarded as the royal—and, usually, the only—road to recovery, it is assumed that more people will get well.

Such optimism overreaches itself. Get well from what? Most often nowadays it is from loneliness, insecurity, doubt, boredom, restlessness, and marital discord. The hysteria of the last century has mysteriously disappeared—as completely as the intolerance with which it was viewed. The tolerant psychoanalyst of today deals rather with vague conditions of maladjustment and discontent. For it has come about that, as the social attitude toward neurosis has changed, the patterns of neuroses have themselves undergone a change of equal magnitude.[6] This is within the personal experience of older psychoanalysts. Younger analysts become aware of it from the discrepancy between the older descriptions of neuroses and the problems presented by the patients who come daily to their offices. The change is from symptom neuroses to character disorders.

A symptom neurosis was understood as a breakthrough in distorted form of a previously repressed impulse. The neurosis appeared as a phobia, an obsession, a compulsion, or as a physical symptom without a physical cause; was characterized by a definite, and often sudden, onset; and occurred in the setting of a relatively well-integrated and adequately functioning personality. It had the quality of a syndrome or illness. Diagnosis was relatively easy. It was the classical indication for psychoanalysis, and with such conditions analysis has had its greatest success. Insight was often quickly effective. Analyses were short, a matter of months rather than years. Such a case has always been considered ideal for teaching purposes, and its current rarity can be attested by almost any analyst in training.

In contrast, the more frequently encountered character disorder of today cannot be adequately understood as the eruption of a previously repressed impulse; for the defensive warping of character is apt to loom larger and prove more troublesome than the erupting impulse. The conflict is less likely to manifest itself in the form of specific symptoms or to have the quality of a syndrome, but is vague and amorphous, pervading the entire personality. Complaints of a general nature become more common, such as, "difficulties in relations with people," "I'm just not very happy, feel I ought to be getting more out of life," or "I'm too rigid." Normality has largely replaced morality as a standard of operational adequacy.[7] The significance of inner conflict to all manner of difficulties in living has been so incontrovertibly established that, for many people, any condition of unhappiness is prima facie evidence of neurosis and hence reason enough to consult a psychoanalyst. Diagnosis becomes increasingly difficult; no one term covers the many things that are wrong; and case reports conclude with formulations of remarkable length and complexity—for example, "reactive depression in a decompensating narcissistic-compulsive character with paranoid, hysterical, and some psychopathic tendencies." With such conditions psychoanalysis is less successful, insight less curative. The analyst speaks less often of "cure" and more frequently of "progress." Analyses become longer, three years and more being quite common; and the time is long past when a second analysis was claim to distinction. The goals of analysis are not fully achieved; both patient and therapist must settle for less than had been hoped for.

THE DECLINE OF WILL

Toward the end of the long analyses that now have become so common, the therapist may find himself wishing that the patient were capable of more push, more determination, a greater willingness to make the best of it. Often this wish eventuates in remarks to the patient: "People must help themselves"; "Nothing worthwhile is achieved without effort"; "You have to try." Such interventions are seldom included in case reports, for it is assumed that they possess neither the dignity nor effectiveness of interpretation. Often an analyst feels uncomfortable about such appeals to volition, as though he were using something he didn't believe in, and as though this would have been unnecessary had only he analyzed more skillfully. The deficiency of will in the patient is mirrored by the loss, in the analyst, of a belief in the efficacy of will. The same culture produces both patient and analyst, and it is a culture in which the strength of individuals is no longer thought to be located in the strength of will.

When human affairs appear to be inexorably determined by forces over which man has no control, the concept of will has little significance. When human affairs are characterized by a sense of freedom, when society concerns itself with the rights and dignity of the individual, the concept of will is of great significance. Since the Renaissance, man's sense of freedom has increased to a point probably unequalled in any prior civilization, achieving such expressions as "I am the master of my fate; I am the captain of my soul." At the same time the material universe was more and more being found to be rigorously determined, more precisely and measurably conforming to natural law. Newtonian mechanics captured the physical sciences for determinism. But, paradoxically, the technological advantages of viewing the universe as "determined" enhanced man's sense of being "free." One cannot build an aeroplane, for example, without allegiance to determinism; yet the creation of an aeroplane tends to support man's sense of standing outside the causal network, of being the master and manipulator of determined events. And so for centuries the inner life of man, the realm of free will, lay outside causality. Even after Darwin captured the biological sciences for determinism there still seemed to be a place for will in human affairs, and as late as 1892

William James maintained that a sense of integrity depends primarily on the ability to will effectively.[8]

More recently the concept of will has passed into partial eclipse. It is still central to those popular books on self-improvement which crowd the best-seller lists; but in psychology it has lost its position as a primary mental function and has become an epiphenomenon. Among the sophisticated the use of the term "will power" has become perhaps the most unambiguous badge of naïveté. It has become unfashionable to try, by one's unaided efforts, to force one's way out of a condition of neurotic misery; for the stronger the will the more likely it is to be labeled a "counterphobic maneuver." The unconscious is heir to the prestige of will. As one's fate formerly was determined by will, now it is determined by the repressed in mental life. Knowledgeable moderns put their backs to the couch, and in so doing they fail occasionally to put their shoulders to the wheel. As will has been devalued, so has courage; for courage can exist only in the service of will, and can hardly be valued higher than that which it serves. In our understanding of human nature we have gained determinism and lost determination—though these two things are neither coordinate nor incompatible.

II ⎰ PSYCHOANALYSIS
⎱ AND
IDEOLOGY

THE CHANGING CONDITIONS OF PSYCHOANALYSIS

The limitations of psychoanalysis [1] as a method of scientific investigation are well known. The absence of controls, the many variables, the uniqueness of each analytic situation, the impossibility of exact measurement—all of these are acknowledged. The analyst maintains, however, that scientific inquiry is a manner of approaching problems and that, though it has flourished most wonderfully in laboratories of controlled experiments and exact measurements, it is not synonymous with such procedures. He holds that even so complex a problem as neurotic suffering may be approached scientifically as opposed to certain other ways, such as traditional, authoritarian, or mystical. He is inclined, indeed, to believe that the hope of human survival lies in the possibility of furthering scientific inquiry into precisely those areas of experience which are least amenable to the methods of exact science, namely morals and the relations between nations.

45

There is, however, another limitation of psychoanalysis as a science which is different in kind and which is less well known: the clinical problems to which it addresses itself are in a process of change. They will not stay put. Analysts often remark upon the evolution of psychoanalysis; they remark hardly ever upon the evolution of its subject matter. In some sense all analysts know that the configurations of neurotic misery are changing; they know, but are reluctant to deal with the implications of this knowledge.

For this reluctance there is a reason. When a problem to the investigation of which one is dedicated is so complex that the work of a lifetime can bring only a partial solution, when the creative work of one man is built on that of his predecessors, and when only the cumulative work of many can possibly achieve understanding and control—when such is the case one needs to believe that it all adds up to something, that the work has not been wasted. One wants, in short, to know that the problem is the same, that it is still real and still challenging. If in the course of this huge labor the problem itself changes, one feels cheated. One can build, and accept the inevitable failures of building, if the ground is firm; but few have the heart to build on earth that is perceptibly sliding into the sea.

In this respect investigators in the physical sciences are on relatively firm ground. Few problems could be more difficult than that of determining the nature of light; but presumably the light emitted by a glowing sodium atom is the same now as when it was first observed. Hence the failures and successes of all able students of this problem are relevant to the scientist who now presses the investigation further. His work is linked to the work of all his predecessors and successors with a continuity that is guaranteed by the sameness of the phenomenon under consideration.

On somewhat less firm ground is the medical man. In the course of time the parasites of man change in nature, the host in vulnerability; and the resulting diseases are subtly or grossly different from those designated by the same name a hundred years previously. The subtle changes, being more easily overlooked, constitute the greater hazard to scientific inquiry. Yet there is much in medicine that meets the need for permanence. Cirrhosis of the liver is likely the same now as in the time of Galen; and under the microscope a carcinoma of the stomach appears the same as it did a hundred years ago, and probably produces the same scatter of consequences.

The psychoanalyst is, in this respect, most poorly situated. He works at the overlapping junction of pathology and normality, an area of such uncertainties that what is called neurotic by one qualified observer may be called normal by the next, treating conditions of unhappiness and discontent that arise from causes as vague and large as life itself. He cannot evade the problem of change by asserting that drives are biologically rooted. They are; but between the biological root and the flowering in experience is interposed a culture in motion. He does not stand on ground at all. His feet are in the currents of social change. And however he may resist, he is in some measure borne along, though he may remain unaware of the drift. It behooves him, however, to become aware. For if, as he charts the shoreline with ever-increasing exactitude, he is unaware of being carried by the current, he will see landmarks that are not there—simply because he has seen them once, or knows them to have been seen by some unimpeachable observer of the past.

The prominent development of psychoanalysis and the obscure evolution in neurotic patterns form a paradoxical concurrence. The emergence of psychoanalysis from nineteenth-century psychiatry was like the transformation of a peasant with a club into a knight with a sword; but in our fascination with the prowess of this new defender we have failed to notice that the dragon has become an enveloping mist. When neurosis had the form of a syndrome or illness it was not received as a respectable malady; now, when it has lost all semblance of a medical entity, it is welcome in the house of medicine. When symptom neuroses were most common, analysis was the struggling outcast of psychiatry; now, when character disorders are most prevalent, analysis is pre-eminent among the psychiatric therapies. The more the unconscious declines in significance,[2] the more confidently do unhappy people come to it in hope. Psychoanalysis was designed, in theory and in practice, to treat the disorders to which the nineteenth-century character was vulnerable, but with that character found no acceptance. It is less well suited to treat the disorders to which the twentieth-century character is subject, but by this character is elevated to high place.

These paradoxical developments are accounted for, in part, by the shift in emphasis from achievement to adjustment. For psychoanalysis offers a unique service to the seeker after adjustment. To him who wishes to interact smoothly and skillfully it is exceedingly important to know how he appears to others, what motives others are noticing in him that he is not aware of presenting for notice. The unconscious has declined in significance but has by no means disappeared. Insofar as it exists at all it renders one vulnerable; for everyone knows that it usually shows to others before it shows to one's self. Constantly one hears persons described—in their absence—as passive or envious or ambivalent, and knows that the person so designated is unaware, if not of the trait itself, then certainly of having displayed it. It behooves one, therefore, to become aware. Psychoanalysis fits this need. Whatever else it does or fails to do, it may be relied on to extend the awareness of one's self and of others.

Psychoanalysis is often criticized for stifling rebellion and encouraging conformity. Though true in certain instances, the charge is generally undeserved. Analysis does not make conformity. It is rather the other way round: conformity is making psychoanalysis—making it one of the most prominent and respected of medical specialties. The drive to adjust is brought by the patient, not inculcated by the analyst.

Yet there is an element of truth in the assertion that psychoanalysis promotes conformity. In its beginnings psychoanalysis was at odds with culture, was critical of social hypocrisies, a challenge to prevailing mores. Society was equally vigorous in its counterattacks. This relationship of psychoanalysis to culture has changed. The tension has diminished. Society now supports psychoanalysis, and psychoanalysis in turn has mellowed. In its time it brought about far-reaching changes, some of which are still being debated. Because of these past achievements it retains the status of critic, but now is emeritus. It is not now a force for cultural change. There is some indication that it may, in fact, become an institutional force for the maintenance of current mores.

But the relation of psychoanalysis to the troubles of modern man is not fully encompassed by the problem of adjustment. Something more is involved. Psychoanalysis has as its proper function the extension of awareness, the making conscious of those things which were unconscious, thereby enhancing one's position in the adjustmental struggle. But when this has been accomplished, many persons are still discontent. Something important, something hoped for, is still lacking. This something more cannot be found in psychoanalysis; for it is not an integrative system, not an ideology. Psychoanalysis provides no value system, nor should it. It has no answer to the confusions of the age. It does not reveal what is worth struggling for or how much.

FAMILY PRAYER

Morris's religion was deeply felt. He believed with a sense of unerring right, and his faith was steadfast. A tenth of his income was given to the church, and though hard times were upon them this tithe was never curtailed. Brother Gibson, the minister, came to see him once or twice a month, and before leaving would always say, "Brother, may I pray for you?" And Morris would say, "I wish you would, Pastor." Whereupon Morris would close his eyes, and the minister would hitch up his pants and kneel on the floor of the porch. He would pray for the quick return to health of "this, Thy devoted son and servant" and for the guidance and protection of "his dear wife, our beloved sister," and would solicit God's loving care for "their dear children."

No meal could begin without a blessing, and when Larry was seven years old this duty was delegated to him. When Morris had been served his meal on a tray, the family would sit down to eat. They ate in the kitchen, and the table was so located that the chair in which Larry sat was visible from the porch. Occasionally Morris would lean out of bed, turn his head, and look at his son. He did this less frequently as he grew weaker, but Larry never knew when he was being watched. When all were seated they would bow their heads and Larry would say grace. He was not permitted to slur it or say it rapidly as a formality, but was obliged to speak reverently in a loud, clear voice, so that his father, as well as God, could hear. "Lord, bless this food that now we take, and make us good for Jesus' sake. Amen." And sometimes from the porch would come a fatherly echo, "Amen." Then they would raise their heads and begin to eat.

Sometimes, however, the end of the blessing would be followed by stinging reprimand. "Sit yourself up straight at that table, sir!" After a moment of bewilderment and fright Larry would realize that he had been slouching in his chair, and would stiffen straightly and wait in silence. "Now you say that blessing again, sir!" He would thus be forced to repeat, and then would falteringly begin to eat, wondering if his father were still watching but afraid to look and find out.

Every night about nine o'clock the family would gather to "talk with God." At this time the work of the day would be done, the dishes washed, the clothes ironed, the floor swept, and the sewing finished. To Caroline it was the most peaceful time of the day. The children would be tired and perhaps sleepy. At this time, in summer, the night would have just arrived, and far away they might hear a train whistle or a dog bark. In winter a woodburning stove would warm the bedroom and porch while the rest of the house would be closed off and cold. Around the corners of the old house would be heard the thrilling, intimate shriek of a norther which had swept down through the flatlands of the great square states, whined through countless barbed-wire fences, across the Panhandle, and so to them. An unshaded bulb, hanging from a yellow, fly-specked cord, would light the room with a soporific glare. Because the underpinning of the house was high and screened only with lattice work, the wind would pass, not only above and around the house, but also under it, lifting the floor boards and making them quiver, and invading the room through the cracks. Sometimes it would get in behind the rain-stained wallpaper, causing it to rattle and flap, and sometimes the house shook so that the room seemed to have lost contact with the ground, and they would have the sensation of being carried away by the wind.

These were the nights when strange noises were heard in the part of the house that was closed off and dark. A door would open and close, the sound of footsteps would come from the adjoining room, and an intruder would stumble against a chair in the kitchen. Tentacles of fear would fasten themselves on

Larry's courage, and Caroline would start with alarm. Then they would look at Morris, see that he was unperturbed, and would know that it was only the tricks of the wind playing with the decrepitude of the time-worn house.

At this time, about nine o'clock in the evening, winter and summer, the family convened for prayer.

When the work of the evening was done, Caroline would sit in her chair on the porch, fold her hands, and wait. Helen and Larry would draw up chairs before the screen door. Then Morris would take up the Bible and begin to turn through the pages. For perhaps five minutes they would sit in silence. This was a time for meditation. Speech and laughter were forbidden.

At this time each evening a familiar feeling of uneasiness would come to Larry. Though family prayer was a daily occurrence, he did not experience the contentment that is supposed to result from communion with God. Rather, when he saw his father open the gilt-edged book and felt the hush and solemnity of worship, he was beset by a sense of insincerity and unworthiness.

After looking meditatively through the Bible for a while in silence, Morris would begin to read aloud—perhaps something from Proverbs.

"My son, forget not my law; but let thine heart keep my commandments: for length of days, and long life, and peace, shall they add to thee. Let not mercy and truth forsake thee: bind them about thy neck; write them upon the table of thine heart: so shalt thou find favor and good understanding in the sight of God and man. Trust in the Lord with all thine heart;

and lean not unto thine own understanding. In all thy ways acknowledge him, and he shall direct thy paths. Be no wise in thine own eyes: fear the Lord and depart from evil. It shall be health to thy navel, and marrow to thy bones. Honor the Lord with thy substance, and with the first fruits of all thine increase: so shall thy barns be filled with plenty, and thy presses shall burst out with new wine. My son, despise not the chastening of the Lord; neither be weary of his correction. For whom the Lord loveth he correcteth; even as a father the son in whom he delighteth."

Slowly he would close the book and look up at his family. "Let us pray."

All of them, excepting Morris, would get down on their knees and bow their heads, resting their arms on the chairs on which they had been sitting. They prayed in a customary order. After kneeling for a few moments in silence, Caroline would begin. She prayed in the soft voice in which she conversed, to which was added on these occasions only a note of humility. She could not mask her feeling, and from the way she spoke Larry would know how she felt. Usually she was calm and self-contained, but occasionally strain and worry would make themselves known by a pleading quality of voice. Rarely she cried. When this happened he would feel a racking shame, and his own eyes would be wet.

"Dear heavenly Father, let the light of Thy blessing shine upon this family tonight. Help us to see Thy way, dear Lord. Make us to know the wisdom of Thy judgments. Not our will, but Thine, be done.

"But, O Lord, if it be Thy will, most humbly do we beseech Thee to restore health to this family. Bring back my husband's strength, dear Lord, that he may carry on Thy fight with renewed vigor, and praise Thy name all the days of his life.

"Bless these our children. May they never stray from the path of righteousness, but follow always in the footsteps of Jesus and strive to do Thy will.

"Forgive us our sins, dear Lord, and have mercy on our shortcomings; for it is in the name of Thy Son, our Savior, Jesus Christ, we ask it. Amen."

Now it was Helen's turn. Unlike Larry, she seemed at ease in the atmosphere of worship.

"Dear heavenly Father, forgive me my sins," she calmly implored. "Help me not to envy my neighbor's possessions or her . . . things."

Larry knew what this referred to. Her best friend, Kathleen Perry, had just been given a formal dress for dances; Helen wanted one like it, but had been refused.

Suddenly he realized that this was no time to be listening to his sister. In a few moments she would be through, and it would be his turn. What would he pray about? What were the words, the tricks of expression, the archaic phraseology with which to achieve a semblance of piety? He had nothing to say to God and would have liked to forego his turn. What would happen, he wondered, if he should say, "Excuse me, please"? Something terrible. Better to patch together an artifact of reverence and speak to the Lord, not from the heart, but from the necessity of circumstance. God, he knew, could differentiate the sincere from the merely professed; but this did not concern him. His efforts were directed toward meeting only those requirements imposed by his earthly father.

What, then, could he say? It was always proper to ask forgiveness for his sins, to ask God's blessing and mercy, and to pray that his father get well. But this could be said very quickly. It was not long enough. He could ask God to make him good, not only in word and deed, but also in thought. That was an old one, but still worth using. He could pray, also, that he be less quick to anger and more willing to forgive those who sinned against him. He could hardly have named a vice from which he was more nearly free than that of losing his temper, and he would have been hard put to name a person who had sinned against him; but it was easier to compose a prayer in cliches than in terms of real sins, shortcomings, and needs. He could ask also that . . . .

But it was too late now! Helen was about to finish. Something in the tone of her voice told him that the sentence now being spoken would be her last, that it would end with the words . . . yes, there they were. ". . . in the name of our Lord, Jesus Christ, Amen."

The room became quiet. They were waiting for him. There was no getting out of it.

"Dear Lord," he began nervously, "forgive us our sins." Here in the house of his everyday life he was standing on his knees with his face in his hands. In a lighted room he had closed his eyes. Having nothing to say, he was speaking insincere words in obsolete phrases to an unseen presence. "Make us to understand Thy meaning and know Thy way. . . ." This had

PSYCHOANALYSIS AND IDEOLOGY

not been planned. It just came out. ". . . and follow Thy path. Help us to forgive our enemies and be kind to those who have sinned against us. Let us be slow to anger, O Lord, and . . . ." Strange how much easier it was, once in the swing of it. ". . . let us always strive to be like our Lord and Savior, Jesus Christ. Give us strength when temptation comes, and help us to do the right thing. Make us good, not only in word and deed but also in thought. Bless Daddy, dear Lord, and make him well. And bless Mama and Helen, and make me a better boy, for Christ's sake, Amen."

It was a great relief to have finished. Moreover, it was a pretty good prayer, he thought. At least he had not troubled the Almighty with such matters as a new dress.

Now the family's most gifted solicitor of heaven began to speak.

"Lord God in heaven, Thou who art so sadly familiar with our misdeeds and limitations, Thou who doth weep when even the least of us doth forsake Thy way and embrace evil, Thou who. . . ."

This voice which, despite invalidism, was forceful and resonant, reverent without being humble, never failed to awe Larry. He felt that his father was closer to God than the rest of them, conversant with Him on more nearly equal terms.

". . . look Thou down upon the miserable shambles of our sin-wrecked lives, O Lord, and be Thou not unmoved by our unhappiness, but let Thy . . . ."

With the familiar thunder of this rhetoric in his ears, Larry could now relax. He could dream or doze or listen, as he chose. Surreptitiously he lowered his rump onto his heels. Such a posture was not permitted at worship; but probably his father could not see him. Anyway, he would take the chance.

". . . purify our hearts with the flame of Thy righteous anger, O God. Spare not Thy rod, but use it to show us Thy way . . . ."

He opened his eyes and looked out narrowly between his fingers. By turning his head slightly he could see his mother's legs extended behind her. They were covered with wrinkled cotton stockings of a tan color. The sole of her right shoe was worn through to the lining, and suddenly this seemed unaccountably pathetic. He thought of her only as being on her feet—coming, going, serving, working—and it was strange to see her in this position, her legs splayed out unnaturally on the floor, the soles of her shoes turned upward, as though she had been injured by violence and were lying unconscious.

". . . Forsake us not in our misdeeds. Be with us always. Let Thy presence be ever felt in our hearts, a beacon in the night of our unworthiness . . . ."

His father's voice rose and fell, giving him a sense of security even though he did not listen.

". . . Purge our minds of evil thoughts . . . ."

Near at hand was his sister, her dark brown hair hanging over her shoulders. She wore a sleeveless nightgown, and he could see her breast. He felt a vague stirring of desire and, with it, unrest.

". . . to us. Bless this family, Thou who knowest all our wants and needs. Grant our just and righteous hopes. Rid us of all designs unworthy of Thy favor. Bring back to us . . . ."

He became absorbed in a phenomenon which had beguiled

many tedious moments of kneeling: looking toward the light with his hands over his eyes he could see through his fingers. They were red and translucent, like apple jelly.

"And if it be Thy will, O Lord, restore my health . . . ."

With their eyes covered, their thoughts following different paths, the family knelt and prayed; and outside the wind moved aimlessly across vast plains.

". . . For Thine is the power, the kingdom, and the glory, for ever and ever, Amen."

SUNDAY

On Sundays the family slept till seven-thirty, an hour later than usual; and breakfast was eaten more leisurely. Larry would then bathe and put on his Sunday clothes. There was plenty of time to read the funny papers, but this was forbidden until after church. At nine the bell would begin to ring, and someone would usually remark, "There goes our bell."

Having missed the sound of church bells, Morris had given his tithe one year in the form of a bell, and thereafter took pleasure in hearing it ring for services on Sunday and for prayer meeting on Wednesday nights. When the bell rang on Sunday morning they would have to hurry, for the church was a mile away and Sunday school began at nine-thirty. Larry was always ready first and would wait impatiently. When his mother appeared to be ready, he knew from experience that she had only begun to dress. Eventually, however, they would say good-bye to Morris and be off. During the first years in Texas Helen had gone too, but as Morris became sicker in the summer of 1924 someone had to stay with him.

Larry was considered too young, Caroline taught a Sunday school class, so usually Helen stayed home.

Upon arriving at Sunday school, Larry would join his class, which met in one corner of the church. It was taught by Mr. Logansberry who, on weekdays, was a plumber. Each child was given a copy of the lesson, a printed and illustrated sheet twice folded and perforated along the left margin so that it might be entered in a looseleaf notebook. The girls saved them, but the boys usually threw them away. The lesson was a Bible story narrated in simple terms. Mr. Logansberry was a kindly person, and a fine man to have around when the pipes were out of order; but with a Bible in his hand he commanded little respect or obedience. The boys threw wads of paper, talked, and tickled or jabbed their neighbors. There were limits, however, and Larry was careful not to exceed them.

After Sunday school came the sermon. The chances of diversion were now reduced to a minimum; few of the children of his age were compelled to stay. Besides, he had to sit with his mother. At this time of day in summer, the church would become oppressively hot; for it was a barnlike structure covered with tarpaper. The walls were unlined and there was no ceiling. The floor was clapboard, and inclined downward from the back of the house to the altar. When it rained and the roof leaked—which it always did—a puddle formed in front of the pulpit. The benches were straight and hard. The church had been built as a temporary measure pending the erection of a stone building, the site for which was already purchased. But this was five years ago, and no sign of the new structure had appeared. The church members numbered about two hundred and fifty, most of whom were poor. It was all they could do to maintain a pastor.

On any Sunday morning a congregation of fifty to seventy-five would sit on the uncomfortable benches in the withering heat and listen to the sermon; and one of them, much against his will, was always Larry. To him the beginning of the service consisted of a tiresome miscellany: reading of the text, collection of the offering, announcements, and the meaningless dialogue of responsive reading. The succession of these items was punctuated by the rising and singing of hymns. Sometimes he would sing loudly, causing his mother to nudge him or, if that were of no avail, to whisper exasperatedly that he was "not to lead the singing." Most of the time, however, he would be silent, and watch the others, or stare moodily at nothing at all. After about fifteen minutes the preliminaries would be finished, and everyone would settle back to listen to the sermon.

So far as he was concerned there were only two kinds of preachers: the kind that spoke gently and quietly, and the kind that started off that way but suddenly got red in the face and began shouting and banging on the pulpit. This church had had its share of both types, and he preferred the former, though he paid little attention to either kind. Occasionally he would listen for a while, particularly if an anecdote were being related. Sometimes he would even be moved. But for the most part he mused idly about indifferent matters, perhaps counting the holes in the roof through which he could see daylight. Every five or ten minutes he would ask his mother if the sermon were about over, and she would whisper: "Yes, just a little while longer. Now be quiet."

Then he would fidget and look at the people around him. Except for his mother's nudgings, he would have turned and looked at those behind him, or got down on the floor and looked under the benches at their feet—anything to pass the time. The preacher would drone on and on. Other possibilities having been exhausted, he would search his pockets for something to play with. Usually his Sunday clothes contained nothing of interest, and he would wish he were wearing his other pants. But even had he found something, his mother would not have let him play with it; for once at an evening service an embarrassing thing had happened. A group of boys were sitting together at the back of the church, talking and creating a disturbance—so much so that the preacher had to interrupt his sermon and admonish them to behave. This quieted them for a while, but soon they were at it again. Then one of them dropped a marble. Everyone heard it fall and heard it start to roll. The pastor stopped speaking, and the church was quiet except for the sound of the marble rolling under the benches on the inclined floor, rapidly gathering speed. No one would have believed it possible that one marble could make so much noise. The pastor's face was flushed with anger. Occasionally the marble would run into one of the benches, bounce, and the rumbling crescendo would begin again. One or two people tried to stop it as it rushed between their feet, but their efforts only added to the irreverence of the scene. Finally it cleared the benches and, with a last burst of speed, traversed the open space and bumped thunderously into the altar. There it bounced back and forth for a while and eventually came to rest. Controlling his wrath, the pastor looked at the sheepish

and snickering miscreants and acidly asked the owner to come
retrieve his marble. No one moved. After glaring at them for
a minute, he tried to resume his sermon, but the presence of
God had been dispelled from that meeting and did not return.

So it was just as well that his pockets contained nothing of
interest. The only things he was apt to find were the Sunday
school lessons for the current and preceding Sundays. Lacking
anything better to do, he would look at the pictures and read
the text again. This was, as a matter of fact, a prudent thing to
do, since on returning home his father would sometimes ask
him about the lesson; and there was no excuse for not knowing.

On and on the sermon would drone and meander, or, if the
minister were of the choleric type, would proceed explosively.
Larry would wait . . . and wait . . . and hope for an ending
until it would seem he had been sitting there always and that
the sermon would go on forever. He would want to slip down
on the bench so as to rest his head against the back, but that
was forbidden. Nor could he draw up his feet and sit cross-
legged, nor lean on his mother's shoulder. Eventually he would
despair and subside into a trance. With his neck constricted by
a tight collar, his metabolism confounded by the heat, the in-
activity, and the exhortation, he would become dizzy and see
things spin before his eyes. Realizing that this perversion of
sensation could be ended by an effort of will, he would not
wish to end it, but would be amused and would preserve the
state of impaired cerebral circulation and its attendant witch-
ery. Now he could see the preacher sail rapidly through the
air, still gesticulating, and disappear out of the window. And
all of the people and benches would sail out after him. With

relaxation of his eye muscles he could see two preachers go sailing by.

If at such a moment Caroline should glance at him she would be chagrined to see his head wagging, his mouth open, his eyes rolling, and a silly grin on his face. Thinking that he was making faces at the minister, she would nudge him sharply and whisper an angry reprimand. He would come out of his daze and the waiting would continue.

Once more he would ask if the sermon were almost finished, and she would purse her lips in displeasure and refuse to answer. He would make an effort to sit still and attend, but after a few minutes would lose the train of thought. Then he would scratch his head and inadvertently touch his ear and that would start him off again. As though previously unaware of this appendage, he would begin to explore it, sticking his fingers into its orifice, following out each groove, and comparing it with the one on the opposite side. Next, he might try to wiggle them, his efforts occasioning contractions of most every muscle in his body except the elusive ones capable of performing the desired movement. A stern glance from his mother would inform him that he was again misbehaving. Feeling that the world was united in solid conspiracy against him, he would try once more to sit still.

Eventually, he would hear the long-awaited words: "Now let us kneel in prayer."

Getting down on his knees would revive him and renew his hope. Often, however, the prayer itself would seem of inordinate length. If, after kneeling for five minutes, there still was no lessening of Brother Gibson's fervor, he would again become restless and listen anxiously for the first words of the Lord's Prayer which usually marked the conclusion. After the prayer the congregation would resume its seats, the choir leader would step forward and announce the hymn, and all would stand to sing. Finally came the benediction, which was the shortest and, to him, the most satisfactory thing ever said in church. With eyes closed and arms outstretched, palms down, the minister would intone: "Now may the grace of God be with you all till we meet again. Amen."

The problem now was getting out of the church. Alone, this could have been accomplished at once, but with his mother it took some time. No sooner were they in the aisle than the dilly-dallying began. Caroline would greet someone, shake hands, comment on the sermon, ask about the other's family, and answer queries about her own. This would be repeated many times as they gradually made their way toward the altar. There, after standing and chatting for a while, she would manage to reach Brother Gibson and would tell him that his sermon was an "inspiring message." The pastor would clasp her hand warmly and hold it for some time, shaking it intermittently. He would ask about Morris, about Helen, and would beam down on Larry and say jovially, "Well, how's this little man?"

"All right, sir."

They would not stay long with the pastor, as others would be waiting to speak to him. They would begin then the long trek toward the exit, making poor headway because of frequent stops. In a brief interval between encounters Larry would plead, "Mama, please let's go on home now!"

And she would reply absently, "All right, hon, we'll go right away."

This might lead to one or two brisk steps, but no more. Someone would again detain them and begin to chat. After ten or fifteen minutes they would be outside the church, and there the diminishing group would stand and talk a while longer. This was the only social life his mother had, but Larry did not know this and would be exasperated by the delay. When at last they would start off together toward home in the glaring heat, they would be tired and hot and thirsty.

Now, however, there was a fine thing to look forward to. On arriving home he would drink a glass of water and, unless his father detained him with questions about the Sunday school lesson, would begin reading the funny papers. Lying prone on the living room floor, he would study them with great care. He would read the dialogue and minutely examine each illustration before going on to the next frame. However tempted, he would not look ahead to discover the ending first. He relished each word and each picture, prolonging its pleasure as long as possible, and this would occupy him for about an hour. The next hour would be given over to Sunday dinner, which was the best meal of the week. When this was over he would dry the dishes as his sister washed them.

Then he would experience a feeling that was to remain with him always as the unique hallmark of holy days—the emptiness and loneliness of Sunday afternoons. It was a feeling that came on gradually. For a while after dinner he would be fairly content, musing over the funny papers, or perhaps reading them again, but soon would feel a stirring of unrest. He would walk through the house, stopping in front of windows and staring moodily outside. Sometimes he would go out and walk around, as if looking for something he knew was not there, then come in again, his loneliness increased. Passing the piano, he would try desultorily to pick out a melody, but soon would tire of his discords. Searching out the members of his family, he would find them engaged in activities alien to his needs.

"Mama, what can I do?" he would ask sadly.

"Well, hon, let me see . . . . Why don't you read a book?" Seeing his face unchanged she might add, "Or why don't you get Helen to play dominoes with you?"

He didn't want to read, Helen didn't want to play dominoes, and his mother had no more suggestions. There was nothing to do on Sunday. If any of his friends had come to see him, he would have been permitted to play some quiet game with them, but they did not come. Their families were not so devout, and they were not interested in quiet games. He was not permitted to visit them; he must stay within the house or its immediate environs. Nor was he allowed to put on old clothes so as to be able to crawl under the house or dig a cave or climb a tree. Sunday was a day for rest and quiet relaxation. But rest he did not need, silence was something of which one could have too much, and relaxation he found impossible within the limits imposed.

Having ascertained that, as he supposed, no unexpected escape was possible, he would act on his mother's suggestion and look for a book. Approaching the bookcase, he would stare morosely at the row of titles behind the glass door. He was familiar with most of them because of similar experiences on past Sundays. Although he had read only a few, he had tried them all and found them dull. The volume to which he most frequently resorted was Dante's *Divine Comedy*, which showed little evidence of ever having been read. There was, however, much to recommend it. He had heard his mother say it was a great book; he knew that comedy was what he most liked; and a divine comedy could hardly be anything other than a superlatively funny one. Therefore, it was usually Dante's work that he eventually drew from the bookcase. He had long since given up the idea of starting at the beginning. He had tried that many times, and there was certainly nothing funny on the first few pages. It was a long book, though; and, assuming that the really funny part came later, he would thumb through the pages, reading a bit here and there, never finding the humor for which he was looking. Not in all the Sundays of his youth did he discover Dante's concealed hilarity, and gradually the book became a symbol of the day itself. For Sunday was as devoid of pleasure and companionship as the *Divine Comedy* was of wit and humor.

Having confirmed his belief that the bookcase contained nothing of interest, he would again wander through the house, or perhaps curl up in a chair and resort to daydreams. The world, he knew, was full of adventure and fun and friendship, were only he free to find them. Someday, he promised himself, he would be free. Then he would do as he liked, search and find, and never be lonely again. Thus would pass the afternoon of the seventh day.

Supper consisted of what was left over from dinner, and

was eaten cold in the quiet kitchen. If Morris were feeling bad they would stay home; but if Caroline felt he could spare her she would again go to church and Larry would be obliged to go with her. Together they would set out just before dark.

The evening service was much like that of the morning, except shorter, more informal, and attended by fewer people. There was, however, a great difference in Larry's attitude toward it. The funny papers had been read, the day was over, and there was nothing to look forward to. Only his feeling of loneliness remained. He was not tempted to misbehave and would sit quietly through the sermon, sometimes listening to what Brother Gibson said, but for the most part hearing the voice only of his own desire. His feelings would merge with those of the songs they sang. All hymns were sad to him and seemed even more so when sung at night by a small congregation in a country church. Looking at the people around him, he would think of all of them as being middle-aged or old, and would suspect that all of them were unhappy. The men were carpenters, plumbers, postmen, grocers, trolley car operators, insurance salesmen, and invalided veterans of the war. The women were housewives. Of what, he would wonder, were they thinking as they stood and sang these hymns? Perhaps of the routine of work to begin again tomorrow. Perhaps of the failure of plans and hopes. The sound of their voices suggested that they had come here to pool their loneliness, to reaffirm their membership in a group, and to be told that all their hardships were manifestations of God's inscrutable plan and that their lives were somehow converging toward an end of eternal happiness.

Sometimes he would glance obliquely at his mother and see her face stroked with sadness as she sang the mournful hymns in a high, sweet voice, always slightly off key.

> Where He leads me I will follow,
> Where He leads me I will follow,
> Where He leads me I will follow,
> I'll go with Him, with Him,
> All the way.

Never throughout his life would he be able to hear these songs without having instantly evoked the feeling of isolation and insecurity as he had known it in the church of his childhood.

As they walked back home in silence through the still night, no light for their steps but the stars, he would resolve to make his life different from those he had seen, to have his happiness here on this earth. He believed that this was possible.

III ⟨ CHARACTER CHANGE AND CULTURAL CHANGE

CULTURE AND SOCIAL CHARACTER

It is generally believed that our changing social character is symptomatic of crisis, that there was a period in the past—the Victorian period, for example—in which character was stable, and that there will be a corresponding period in the future in which society will have emerged from its present chaos, when stable traditions will again foster a stable character. The troubles which seem most crucial to an observer of any period are the troubles of his present; those receding into the past he views with detachment. The biggest wave is the one now striking the ship; toward the horizon, ahead or astern, the sea is level. And so our present, with its troubles and uncertainties, is seen as a temporary and perilous transition.

This belief will not bear scrutiny. Clearly character cannot remain fixed while the conditions of life change. And clearly the conditions of life have always been changing. Any culture tends to produce in individuals that social character which is fitted for survival in that culture;[1] and as a culture evolves, an evolution in the prevailing character of the individuals who adapt to it is to be expected. That there should have been a characterological change of some kind in western society during the past two generations occasions no surprise, nor should it. For the conditions of life have, during that time, undergone such radical alteration that it would be a greater mystery if no corresponding change in character had occurred. We know this in the same way we know that the Norman conquerors, the imperial Romans, the fabled Babylonians, and the stone age men must have been characterologically different, each from the others and each from ourselves. Since evolution has been intrinsic to culture for as long as we have any knowledge of culture, character, also, must always have been in a process of change.

Radical changes in the circumstances of life may befall man, as the several ice ages doubtless brought about different ways of life for peoples of the northern hemisphere. Such changes have, in the period of recorded history, become progressively less important: the changes brought about by man himself have provided the major problems of adaptation. It is the nature and continuity of these changes that are in question here.

THE INSTITUTIONAL PROCESS AND THE INSTRUMENTAL PROCESS

It is not possible to view the life of man apart from culture; for there is no man whose life has not been shaped from birth to death by its cultural matrix. An approximation of the life of man without culture is afforded by those animals most closely related to man. Their lives consist of being born, eating, sleeping, playing, fighting, mating, procuring food, caring for young, and dying. All of these activities continue in the life of man, and are the life process for him as they are for other species. But in man—even the most primitive man—these activities are shaped by two superimposed modes of action which are distinctively human. These are the use of tools and the creation of myths. Culture is the product of these modes, and the distinction between them establishes the concepts with which culture may be analyzed and understood. These concepts were first indicated by Veblen, and have been elaborated and clarified by Dewey and Ayres. They are the instrumental process and the institutional process. Each of them encompasses a vast range of phenomena, yet they bear a precise meaning.

The instrumental process designates those activities dominated by an attitude which, if put in words, would be somewhat as follows: "Let us first examine the facts, and draw only such conclusions as the facts warrant. If no conclusion is warranted but some conclusion is necessary—since life does not wait on certainty—then let us hold the conclusion tentative and revise it as new evidence is gathered." Scientific method, therefore, approximates the essence of the matter; but the instrumental process is a larger concept. The origin of scientific method falls within recorded history, but the instrumental process is as old as man. It was a momentous event in this process when one of our remote forebears discovered by accident that fire can be maintained indefinitely by adding dry wood; but few persons would care to label this as science. The continuum of tools extends unbroken from the first flint knife to the latest atom-smasher, and this continuum is at the very heart of the concept; but, again, the instrumental process designates something more. Technology is usually taken to mean material artifacts, but the discovery and use of conceptual tools is an essential part of the instrumental process. It includes the differential calculus as well as the flying machine, the diatonic scale as well as the microscope. It includes, also, art, both fine and applied. For art, as all artists know, is a problem-solving activity in which answers are achieved by taking pains, not by revelation from on high or seizure by a muse. This is not to deny the existence or importance of chance insight or inspiration, either scientific or artistic; but chance, as Claude Bernard has remarked, favors the prepared mind. The authority of the instrumental process is rational, deriving from its demonstrable usefulness to the life process. The final appeal is to the evidence.

The institutional process designates all those activities which are dominated by the quest for certainty. Everything mundane is subject to change, and hence certainty is not to be found in the affairs of men. The searcher arrives at his goal, therefore, in a realm of being superordinate to man. Solomon put it succinctly: "Trust in the Lord with all thine heart; and lean not unto thine own understanding." Religion conveys the essence, but the institutional process is of greater scope. Religion was a relatively late development in the institutional process, as scientific method was a relatively late development in the instrumental process. Far older are animism and the alleged omnipotence of thought, which is magic. With these go rites, taboos, mores, and ceremonial compulsions. All of these belong to the institutional process and are part of a continuum which includes kingship, status, and the coercive power systems of such modern institutions as private property and the sovereign state. The authority of the institutional process is arbitrary; the final appeal is to force.

The instrumental process is bound to reality. Facts are facts, it seems to say. Ignoring them is of no avail. One doesn't have to like them, but he who would gratify his needs and secure himself from peril had better take them into account. Reality can be altered, particularly if it is closely observed. Indeed, the better one understands it and the more tools one has to deal with it, the more radically it can be changed. But it's there, for better or for worse, and the only way to make it better is to attend to it. The instrumental process is generally disparaged as mere problem-solving; for the security it creates, though real, is limited.

The institutional process is bound to human desire and fear. Wishing will make it so, it seems to say. It is unbearable that no one should care; so there must exist a heavenly Father who loves us. Activities of the institutional process do not, objectively, gratify any need or guard against any danger; incantation does not cause rain to fall or game to be plentiful. But such activities may engender a subjective sense of security, and this has always been a fact to be reckoned with—and, indeed, to be exploited. Honor and prestige accrue to the institutional process; for the security it creates, though illusory, is unlimited.

THE INDIVIDUAL AND THE SOCIAL

Freud has described a mode of mental functioning, motivated by needs, which tolerates no deferment of gratification. The needs constitute an imperative which reality must meet or before which reality must give way. If the need-gratifying object is not immediately at hand it will be created in fantasy or by hallucination. This mode of mental functioning is characteristic of the unconscious, is apparent in dreams, and may be observed in the behavior of infants. Freud called it the primary process. It is to a greater or lesser degree replaced in the course of growth and development by another mode of mental functioning of which rational thought is an example. This mode, too, is motivated by needs, but the needs no longer constitute an imperative. Allegiance is given to reality as well, and the needs no longer warrant the fantasied creation or destruction of fact. This mode of mental functioning is characterized by tolerance of delay, attention to reality, detour activities, and compromise solutions. Freud called this the secondary process.

Clearly there is a striking parallel between the primary and secondary processes at the individual level of analysis, and the institutional and instrumental processes at the cultural level of analysis.

Such a correspondence appears to make possible the analysis of culture in terms of mental functions. Freud, for example, viewed culture as "a product of three independent variables: (1) necessity . . . imposed by nature; (2) the instinctual polarity in man: love and death . . . and (3) the institutions and ideals developed by society." [2] These concepts are not, however, coordinate, but refer to different levels of generalization. Scarcity is not an independent variable, but a function of the state of the industrial arts. Wild game was once the principal natural resource, but is so no longer. Arable land was hardly a natural resource before the discovery of agriculture. Coal became a natural resource only with the advent of tools with which it could be dug from the ground and of furnaces in which it could be used as fuel. And uranium has become a natural resource only in our own generation. Scarcity, therefore, has no meaning except as defined by a prevailing technology.

The instinctual drives of man are not a variable at all, but a constant. There is no evidence that they have changed in the course of man's known history, that a Carthaginian general was instinctually any different from an American businessman. The structural and instinctual nature of man would have to be invoked to explain why man creates civilizations, whereas apes do not; and without doubt any further evolutionary change in man's biological endowment would have profound effects on culture. With equal obviousness no society could long endure which wholly thwarted human needs. Any society which enforced exceptionless sexual continence or exacted the sacrifice of all newborn infants would cease to exist within a generation. But instinctual drives do not determine the patterns of culture; it is culture that determines the patterns of instinctual drives. To the problem of cultural change instinctual drives are irrelevant, bearing the same relationship as does the law of gravity to the discovery and progress of aviation. The constant of biologically given needs cannot, therefore, explain the pageant of successive and diverse cultures in which these needs have achieved varying gratifications and suffered varying frustrations.

The frustration of human needs imposed by a culture may,

of course, provide a starting point for the criticism of that culture. But if such criticism is to initiate cultural change it must proceed from the level of instinctual protest to the level of cultural process. It must enter, specifically, the instrumental process. The entire body of Freud's work is a landmark in this process and has thus been a force for cultural change.

Cultural change is a product of cultural forces. The analysis of this process, therefore, requires concepts on this level of generalization.

The separation of human activities into instrumental and institutional categories creates a dichotomy. As Ayres has pointed out, however, it does not create a dualism. It does not establish two realms of being, such as mind and body, but designates distinct aspects of a single and continuous life process. Both are present at all times. Both call upon and give expression to the entire range of human faculties. Both minister to human needs, in fact or in fantasy. In most human endeavors the two aspects are intricately interwoven. The governing of a state, for example, includes countless activities dominated by status and precedent, existing side by side with equally numerous processes of matter-of-fact problem-solving.[3]

THE DYNAMIC OF CULTURAL CHANGE

The dynamic of cultural change is not to be found in politics, conquest, or revolution. Events in these areas are the visible expressions of a process of change that takes place continuously, and for the most part without notice, in the instrumental process. Acceleration is intrinsic to this process. The devices which transform man's environment—whether they be material, as the automobile, or intellectual, as the differential calculus—proliferate by geometric progression. The more tools in existence, the more new tool-combinations are possible. The introduction of keels into a culture that contains sails and rudders is likely to yield sailing ships. The perfection of an internal combustion engine by a culture that contains buggies and kites will certainly result in automobiles and airplanes. A historical chart of such devices, therefore, has the appearance of a logarithmic graph: the entries become most crowded together as one approaches the present.[4] This principle does not, of course, assert that the technological achievements of 1960 will be more numerous or more significant than those of 1950; its applicability is to time spans of greater length. Nor does it assert that the technological process is an imperative. Coercive institutional power may retard it, may, indeed, bring it to a complete stop, as is evidenced by the continuing existence of stone age culture in some parts of the world. Its validity is as a principle rather than a law. It asserts only that the instrumental process possesses an inherent dynamic of accelerating progression.

With these reservations, the principle fits the facts both of historical information and of contemporary observation. Of those periods of culture which are defined by the existing technology, the older the period the greater its length. The old stone age, for example, endured for a million years. The new stone age, brief in comparison, was still of a duration greater than all subsequent time. And in the "Dark" Ages—when, according to the old history books, the culture of Christendom was static—there were beginning to appear in western Europe those devices which prepared the way for the industrial revolution to follow—printing, gunpowder, the compass, the astrolabe, the symbol for zero, the mill wheel, and the clock.[5] At any time in the history of man the rate of technological development was greater than it had ever previously been; at present it is the fastest known.

The instrumental process, therefore, is the source of cultural change. This is not to deny that it might be maintained with equal truth that the source of change lies in the spirit of man that soareth upward; but it is in precisely such instrumental activities that the soaring and Promethean spirit of man is evidenced. For the instrumental process denotes, not only the material concatenation of devices and machines, but all of the problem-solving activities of the investigative and creative mind of man.

As change is the essence of the instrumental process, so standing pat is the essence of the institutional process. Institutions change only under duress, only under the impact, direct or remote, of the instrumental process. Revolutionary changes are implicit in the discovery of fire, agriculture, the wheel, and printing from movable type; but no impetus to change is to be found in the institutions of private property, the church, the divine right of kings, or human sacrifice to gods.

Institutions do, however, expand. They are coercive power systems, and they extend their authority to the furthest possible reach. The history of nations and of religions is a record of such expansions, their ebb and flow. The force of institutions, however, is unalterably opposed to developments in the instrumental process which give a new direction to culture and thereby threaten institutional authority.

Nevertheless institutions usually claim credit for those cultural changes which, in retrospect, seem to have been desirable. Capitalism, for example, is said to have made possible the industrial revolution; and the church is said to have made possible the colonization of the new world. Such claims—and these are representative—do not bear examination. The industrial revolution was the outcome of an advancing technology, particularly of power machinery which made large-scale productive operations more feasible than ever before. To the institution of capitalism belongs the credit only of not having halted the process, of having been permissive of its development. The Catholic Church certainly was active in converting the natives of New Spain; likewise the Spanish soldiers were active in plundering. The colonization of the new world might be credited with equal plausibility to the greed of individuals or nations, to the love of adventure, or to any other activity or motive evidenced by the colonists. Such claims proliferate easily, but miss the point. European settlements in the new world were a function of ships which could undertake Atlantic crossings. Without such ships there could be no settlements; with such ships it was only a matter of time until settlements were undertaken.

CULTURAL LAG

The instrumental impetus to change and the institutional insistence on rooted permanence constitute the dialectic of civilization. These contrary tendencies generate a growing discrepancy between technology and institutions and, consequently, a mounting social tension. Institutions change under the impact of technological progress. They change slowly and reluctantly, but they do change and make peace, finally, with the conditions which altered them. By then technology has moved on, and the laggard is still trailing. The discrepancy remains, only its position has shifted. This is the phenomenon of cultural lag. As a social problem it becomes increasingly crucial, because the lag itself increases. For, while technological progress is an accelerative progression, institutional malleability undergoes no such increase. Institutional practices, therefore, become progressively more at variance with the industrial arts.

The sovereign national state, for example, had become anachronistic by 1914. Developments in transportation and communication, in production and commerce, had rendered it dangerously at odds with industrial civilization. But though obsolete in principle, it was—and still is—very much alive. In the intervening forty-odd years sovereignty has been but minimally curtailed, while technological progress has veritably transformed the world. The discrepancy has consequently increased.

At times the discrepancy between institutions and technology becomes an incompatibility, and then one or the other must give way. The relatively straightforward course of western civilization during the past two thousand years is an indication that institutions have usually given way; but we have no guarantee that such will continue. If, as seems likely, the discrepancy between national sovereignty and prevailing technology has already become an incompatibility, and if this issue should be decided by force, we are in no way assured that it would be the institution of national sovereignty that would be destroyed. It might be—as we are frequently warned—industrial civilization itself which would disappear. Such a possibility lends unique urgency to the issue of cultural lag in our time.

SOCIAL CHARACTER AND THE INSTRUMENTAL PROCESS

Change in social character is to be related to change in the conditions of life; and change in the conditions of life is to be traced to the instrumental process. If these propositions are true, the emergent social character and the problem of identity must in some way correspond to the emergent consequences of the instrumental process. The nature of this correspondence, however, is not immediately clear. For social character is not fashioned out of the primary impact of technological change. Character is not molded by gadgets. New industrial procedures and scientific concepts do not directly alter personality.

The immediate causes of the characterological change are to be found in the secondary effects of technological change: the loss of the eternal verities and the fixed order, the weakening of traditions and institutions, the shifting values, the altered patterns of personal relationships. These changes directly mold character, and these changes occur with a continuity that is traceable to the continuity of the instrumental process.

Yet the belief that social character was formerly fixed and stable contains at least two elements of truth. The first of these is that character is now changing faster than it did in the past, a difference in rate that is easily mistaken for a difference in state. The second is that, during most of human history, change in the character of a people has proceeded so slowly as to be imperceptible during its occurrence. What is new is not the fact that social character is changing; this has always been in process. What is new is its occurrence at a more rapid rate than ever before and, thereby, our awareness of the change as it is taking place.

IV $\left\{\begin{array}{l} \text{THE EMERGENT} \\ \text{SOCIAL} \\ \text{CHARACTER} \end{array}\right.$

POISED TO CHANGE

The social character now coming to prevail seems sculptured to fit a culture of change. In order to survive, it would appear that the individual must become progressively more able to modify himself, to alter his values, to change his reactions. The currently developing social character is equipped with precisely this potential. In it the light touch supplants the firm grip; the launcher of trial balloons replaces the committed man. One avoids final decisions, keeps everything subject to revision, and stands ready to change course when the winds change. The key words of our time are flexibility, adjustment, and warmth—as, for our grandfathers, they were work, thrift, and will.

Nevertheless, this character may not be best fitted for survival. That it exists at all is proof that it can survive in the present; that it is coming generally to prevail is proof that strong and widely-felt forces are participating in its formation. But these facts do not establish either that it is the only configuration of social character that could survive in the present or that, of all possible configurations, it is the one best fitted for survival, either in the present or in the long run. The social character which came to be dominant in Rome in the fourth century A. D. was quite possibly not the one best fitted for the survival of either the groups that exemplified it or the culture that formed it.

This is not to foretell disaster, but only to indicate that the characterological creations of culture are not necessarily most apt even for the culture that creates them. The fact that culture produces social character by the operation of pervasive and subtle influences that are superordinate to the conscious intent of individuals—a process which acquires thereby the status of an automatic mechanism—warrants no assumption of either purpose or infallibility. Cultures as well as individuals are full of automatic mechanisms that at times go dreadfully awry.

It might be inferred that a character fashioned by social conditions which require plasticity of character would not pursue distant goals. For goals, being the manifest expression of character, can hardly remain fixed while the character which they define changes. And what might be inferred can indeed be observed. The social character that is coming to prevail is not given to dedicated pursuits.[1] As the preoccupation with adjustment has increased, the drive for achievement has diminished. Idealism is on the wane; for the ideal, however variously conceived, is always at considerable distance from the actual. It is becoming more rare to believe, individually, with such conviction as to be willing, if necessary, to die for one's belief.

To commit allegiance and will and energy to valued ends means to define the self in terms of these ends and to find in them the enduring meaning and purpose of life. The social character of our time, being largely without goals, lacks this sense of meaning and purpose. This lack is experienced as futility, emptiness, and longing. It forms a reservoir of restless energy which seeks attachment, presses for discharge. It is the explosive fuel for, among other things, mass movements.[2] For when, from time to time, the level rises above a critical point, there appears a leader who can define a goal and force its acceptance, can exact allegiance, command the free energy, and can thereby give meaning to life and dispel the feeling of futility. Then one does have something for which he is willing to die. It is coming to be characteristic of our time that only in mass movements do goals become vital and vitalizing. The identity which is defined by their pursuit is firm and sharply circumscribed, but is not individually achieved. It is stamped out in millions by the modern production techniques of fanatic ideology.

Without meaningful goals modern man has, understandably, no sense of direction; for he does not look where he is going. Like an anxious soldier on a drill field he covertly watches those around him to make sure he stays in step. He sticks to the group, and where the group will go next nobody knows. He despairs of its zigzag course, but hesitates to strike out on his own in any direction because of the likelihood that no one direction can be long maintained. He adjusts to the group and keeps in step and executes the increasingly frequent maneuvers with increasing alacrity. Poised to wheel and turn, he pursues no ends, but rather perfects the instrument of achievement, his personality, which is kept flexible, alert, and perceptive. His character acquires a fine readiness for some unknown undertaking to which it is never committed. He is burdened by a sense of futility and longs for something or someone to give meaning to his life, to tell him who he is, to give him something to live for.

Emergent social tasks are everywhere at hand, and the great social tasks of the past are still unfinished. Rousseau's stinging challenge, "Man is born free, and everywhere he is in chains," retains some pertinence for us after two hundred years. The old verities are still available, but may be found in libraries more readily than in the hearts of living men. They provide no answer for the man of today, and so make no valid claim on his allegiance. The religion of his parents has lost all meaning for him; the Marxism of his youth has become fatuous as well as dangerous. His grandfather was determined to blaze a trail, to become rich, to build a railroad, or to create a farm out of the wilderness. The grandson is not very interested in these things, or in their modern equivalents. He has become weary and skeptical. He is not seeking some *new* value; it is not novelty he needs, but durability. He is a seeker after something that will provide what values and goals have always provided; but he wants it to be different in kind. For values, he feels, cannot be made to stay. Their change is forced by a changing world, and he wants something that will last. But what can substitute for values except other values? What can function as goals except other goals? And on what basis could any possible value or goal be exempt from the engulfing flux?

There is, indeed, no escape from values and goals, or from their vulnerability. There is nothing different in kind but same in function. The effort to diminish the stress occasioned by accelerating change cannot eliminate goals and values. It can, however, force them to become subjective. One abandons the tasks of the world and bends one's efforts upon one's self. One gives up hope of changing the world and resigns one's self to the alteration only of one's reactions. This is the current guise of defeat. One seeks adjustment, a flexible personality, warm interpersonal relationships; and most particularly one cultivates an increasingly sensitive awareness of one's inner life and conflicts. But the energies of man drive for discharge; the direction of flow is outward. The cultivation only of one's self can command but a small fraction of one's potential motivation. The larger part remains dammed up, a reservoir of restless discontent.

HOMOGENEITY, HETEROGENEITY, AND CONFORMITY

Observations of this kind have led to the designation of our time as an age of conformity, and our culture as one of increasing homogeneity. There is much to support this view. Traveling across the continent one sees a striking sameness. From Florida to Oregon people live in the same ranch style or tract houses, wear the same variety of clothes, read the same books, magazines, and editorials, see the same movies and television programs, listen to the same newscasts, discuss the same issues. From Tucson to Stockbridge they drive the same cars along the same superhighways, through towns which look alike, past the same billboards extolling the same beer, stop at the same motels, eat the same foods, use the same toothpaste, and go to sleep on the same foam-rubber mattresses. The traveler of fifty years ago would have found more diversity. From New England to the Oklahoma territory he would have observed striking differences in food, clothes, houses, recreation, education, manners, morals, customs, law and order. Most of those things which tend now toward uniformity were then diverse. This homogeneity is frequently cited as evidence of a growing need to conform. It is said that we, as individuals, are trying harder than ever to be like everybody else, that we are losing the potential for rebellion, for finding our own unique way in life.

The observations of homogeneity are beyond question, but in terms of individual experience they miss the point. For any individual the cultural change has been in precisely the opposite direction—from a relative homogeneity fifty years ago to a bewildering heterogeneity today. The apparent paradox is produced by a shifting point of view. It is only from a vantage point which scans the life of the entire country that the culture of fifty years ago appears heterogeneous; the vantage point of individuals living at that time permitted no such sweeping view. Their cultural horizons included but little more than the regions in which they lived, and within these limits the culture was relatively homogeneous. Technological change has since pushed back these horizons, has brought the culture

of New York, Detroit, and Hollywood to people living any-
where in the land.

As the culture as a whole has become more uniform, the
culture that impacts on any individual has become more diverse. The very changes that have brought about an over-all
sameness to American life have enormously increased the variety of influences that play on the individual. As the culture
as a whole gains in unity, the individual has a harder time
maintaining a sense of personal unity and wholeness.

The present homogeneity of American life does not reflect
a heightened tendency to conform. The observed facts are
clearly a function of technological change, particularly the
revolution in communication, transport, and mass production.
If there has been any actual change in the tendency to conform, it is more likely to have decreased; for experience now
is pluralistic, and choice is presented in areas that formerly
permitted of only one course of action. The striking feature
of present-day American life is precisely that there is no one
over-all mode of conduct. As Daniel Bell has remarked, "One
would be hard put to it to find today the 'conformity' *Main
Street* exacted of Carol Kennicott thirty years ago." [3] School
teachers are still well advised to be discreet in their personal
relations, but surely they have a little more leeway now than
in 1900.

The issue is not a change in the tendency to conform, but a
change in the experienced value of what is conformed to. In
the last century a person growing up in a small American
town experienced a relatively homogeneous society. The

cultural boundaries were close at hand and the life they circumscribed was of a piece. The prevailing manners, morals, and customs were of stable value and were usually accepted without question. They provided the basis for the sense of identity. They defined—not one way of life among many—but *the* way of life, the right way. Following this way of life insured basic security. The approval of others was desirable, but not necessary. Conformity was more nearly automatic.

Today the village society has been replaced by the mass society. However small the town in which one lives, one's world is nevertheless expanded. Being exposed to heterogeneous manners, customs, and morals, their relativity can no longer be ignored. Eternal verities become mores. *The* way of life comes to be but one way among many. A fixed order of final truth has become a relative order of expedient truth. One conforms to some segment of this relative order, but conformity yields diminished security. The approval of others becomes essential. The perceived relativity of mores has diminished their experienced value.

Conformity may not have changed in degree, but our awareness of it has increased, and this entails a change in quality. Formerly it was not experienced as conformity at all, but rather as adherence to principle. One did not "conform" to the right way of life; one rather "elected"—proudly and with "free" will—to be honorable and upright. These categories did not appear to be defined by mores, but by divine revelation or self-evident truth. Today conformity is experienced more largely as such—namely, as adherence to custom. The change detracts from self-esteem as well as from security.

Conformity to Southern Methodism was apt to yield a sense of righteousness; conformity to the *avant garde* is apt to yield a lurking sense of opportunism.

The change from coherent to conflicting mores accounts in large measure for the extended awareness of one's self and of others that is characteristic of the emergent social character. In a homogeneous society those motivations which run counter to mores are more apt to be excluded from individual awareness—as deviant sexual impulses were more apt to be repressed in Victorian society. In a heterogeneous society such repression is less likely. Not one way of life is offered, but many—and many of them incompatible. One conforms to those patterns which seem most appropriate, but continues to be exposed to diverse other influences. The mores that seem alien appeal to repressed motivations and facilitate the emergence of these motivations into consciousness.

This same change accounts, also, for the fact that it is becoming rare to value any belief more than life. To be willing to die for a belief means to be unable to conceive of an acceptable life outside the framework of that belief. The pluralistic and heterogeneous quality of present-day experience undermines such exclusive beliefs; for such a variety of values, standards, and ways of life are presented that no one of them seems indispensable. One *can* conceive of a tolerable life outside the framework of any ideology, and so is unwilling to die for any of them. In a mass movement, however, homogeneity may again be achieved, at least temporarily. The ideology may define the only acceptable life, and martyrdom again becomes possible.

MORES AND MORALS

Mores are usually distinguished from morals. "What is customary?" makes reference to mores. "What would be right?" makes reference to morals. Indeed, the difference in the verb form in these two questions indicates something of the difference between the subjects. Mores refer to the present, morals to all time. In morals one is not concerned with practice, but with principle.

Upon scrutiny, however, the principle proves to have originated in practice and to have a personal origin. The moral decision is the one which would be reached by a wise person of the past, were he in the same situation. This wise person, when exposed, usually turns out to be a parent—or a composite of both parents, and perhaps other older persons who were important in one's childhood. In reaching a moral decision, however, one does not usually make conscious reference to the person from whose practice the principle was derived; one makes reference only to the residue of that person which exists within one's self. This is one's conscience, a distillate of the past, the bearer of tradition. It is what one feels to be the best of his past, that most worthy of being preserved and honored. To act morally is to act in conformity to this residue of the past, even though such action be at odds with prevailing practice.

Mores, therefore, refer to prevailing practice, and the issue is one of adjustment. Morals refer to principles derived from the past, and the issue is one of integrity. This is the way the matter seems when viewed from within the confines of any culture. The distinction seems clear: what is customary is secular and temporary and relative; what is right is transcendent and permanent and absolute.

When, however, one views the same issue from the vantage point of a different culture, the distinction fades. Morals are seen to be simply the more durable mores, the mores which that particular culture deems most important. Sexual fidelity in marriage is, for us, a matter of morals; putting on one's best clothes to go to church, a matter of mores. One is a matter of right and wrong, the other a matter of custom. But from the vantage point of a different culture both practices are seen to possess only the same sanction: they are customary for our culture.

Mores, therefore, define what is right as well as what is customary. They establish what is worth striving for, cherishing, and protecting. And the authority of mores is simply that they exist. They are what they happen to be, and that is all they are. They possess no transcultural validity. They are the guiding agencies of life for those who are guided by them— and for none others. Billions of words have been written, and millions of persons have died, for the purpose of establishing a higher authority for mores, an authority rational or divine in nature, absolute in certainty, universal in scope, and eternal in duration; but the lives were wasted and the words are convincing only to those who already believe. The ineluctable fact is that the validity of mores is relative to the culture that supports them. The values that derive from them are likewise relative.

Moral behavior, therefore, is culturally relative and is defined by the mores. In any situation one will be acting morally if he acts as the "best" people of that culture act in that situation.[4] The "best" people are, of course, those of highest status. One who acts contrary to the most valued mores is immoral. If such action should lead to the downfall of existing mores and to the establishment of new ones, he may become known to later generations as a great moral leader. But at the time of the violation he is judged immoral. Moral behavior, therefore, is essentially imitative.

Since morals derive from mores, moral values are institutional in nature. There is no reason why they must necessarily be institutional; it is simply a matter of fact that they usually are. Instrumental values are relegated to an inferior realm. Indeed, if one performs a "good" act because of its demonstrable instrumental value, the act is not considered truly moral; it has, for most persons, the flavor of opportunism. Honesty is the best policy, we say; and this is an assertion of instrumental value. But we don't really expect people to be honest *because* it's the best policy. We expect them to be honest because it's *right*, and to console themselves for losses which the exercise of this virtue may entail by recalling that, in addition to being right, it is said to be to their advantage in the long run. Whenever we encounter a person who is honest only because he believes honesty to work to his ultimate advantage, we are apt to consider him morally inferior to one who is honest because of a belief that honesty is "right" in an absolute and transcendental sense.

In morals we hesitate to trust the processes of intelligent

inquiry, fearing that our matter-of-fact considerations will be inadequate, that our purview of relevant facts will be short-range and misleading. Actually we believe that most of our morality has instrumental value, that its demonstrable consequences will be individually and socially beneficial. But we are loath to let it rest on that basis. For if it had no other sanction, then it would be open to question and to critical scrutiny. Alternate hypotheses would be formed, experiments undertaken; and when such processes get underway, change is certain. The changes might be to our great advantage, but we are afraid to risk it. We try to secure the good by making it an absolute, by placing it in a realm beyond the reach of intelligent inquiry. In this way morality is divorced from the instrumental process.

EGO AND SUPEREGO

Though moral behavior is essentially imitative, it is not operationally imitative. In reaching a moral decision the inner experience is one of determining the application of basic principles to a unique situation. It is not important that the action to ensue be in accord with the behavior of contemporaries, but that it be in accord with eternal verities. Morality acquires this judicial and reflective quality by virtue of conscience, which is formed by the incorporation within the child of parental attitudes. These parental attitudes, having themselves been formed in the same way, reflect the mores. They reflect, specifically, those mores which society deems most important, those upon whose continuing integrity the continuance of orderly social life is thought to depend. Conscience becomes, therefore, the repository and the guardian of these mores. It is the carrier of tradition and the foe of change.

The executive department of personality is known as the ego. It is a cohesive and more or less integrated group of functions; it is the locus of perception, evaluation, anticipation, and decision; it is largely, but not altogether, conscious. Impelled by basic needs and heedful of the strictures of conscience, it is the function of the ego to remain in touch with reality, to take note of changing conditions, to seize opportunities for gratification and security, and to initiate change in order to facilitate gratification and security.

The judicial department of personality is called the superego. What has been said of conscience could be said also of the superego; for conscience is part of the superego. Superego, therefore, is the more inclusive concept, being related to conscience as a whole is related to a part. Conscience may enter awareness; the superego is largely unconscious. Of conscience one may say that it carries into the present that which one feels to be the best of the past, that most deserving of being preserved and honored. Of the superego, particularly its unconscious aspects, one would have to say that it also carries into the present that which was most coercive and threatening in the past. The superego acts as a governor to the ego, administering both praise and blame, reward and punishment. It requires the ego to hew to the line, to keep its eye on eternal verities. Upon occasion it compels the ego to ignore opportunities for the safe gratification of impulse, forbids it to take advantage of changed conditions. Its dictum to the ego is, "What was good for your forefathers is good enough for you."

The ego is the agency of change and adaptation; the superego is the carrier of tradition and the defender of mores.

At the psychological level of analysis, therefore, the ego and the superego parallel with curious exactness the instrumental process and the institutional process at the cultural level of analysis. This observation leads directly to a hypothesis: A society in which the prevailing social character is marked by a superego with authority of wide scope will offer relatively vigorous institutional opposition to technological change; and, conversely, a society in which the prevailing social character is marked by a superego with authority of diminished scope will offer diminished institutional opposition to technological change. Since technological change has flourished in America during the past fifty years as never before, this hypothesis would suggest that the change in social character during this period has involved a change in the superego. It suggests, specifically, that the superego has become weaker—either by diminished authority within its realm or, more probably, by a shrinking of the realm over which it exercises authority—and that the control of impulse now devolves more largely upon the ego. It is to the investigation of these propositions that the inquiry now proceeds.

THE DECLINE OF THE SUPEREGO

Prior to the formation of the superego a child may refrain from a forbidden act because of the likelihood of being apprehended and punished; after its formation he will refrain because the act is "wrong." The rein on impulse is thereafter held by an agency within his own personality. The superego becomes relatively autonomous, functions largely on its own steam. Occasionally its autonomy in reference to other aspects of personality may be absolute, as when one elects to lose his life rather than betray his principles. But martyrdom is rare; usually the superego is only relatively independent, leaning heavily upon external support. This support is likely to remain unnoticed so long as it is continued. Only when it is lost does its extent and significance become manifest.

One who lives out his life in the town of his birth derives much superego support from proximity to family and relatives, and from their continuing expectations of him. They know what kind of person he is, and they expect him to continue being that kind of person. If the culture of the community is relatively homogeneous, conscience is strengthened also by the continuing pattern of known traditions, customs, and values. Unopposed mores are not subject to critical scrutiny, but are taken for granted. They comprise *the* way of life. The continuance in parents and in the community at large of the way of life from which the superego was derived continues to nourish and strengthen that superego. Life under such conditions is orderly and predictable.

Such conditions are becoming increasingly rare. Few persons these days live out their lives in the place of their birth or in proximity to parents. We move about the continent and, indeed, the world, with increasing freedom and speed; and such superego support as was formerly had from the continued presence of those persons from whom the superego was derived has been largely withdrawn. Immigrants have often been astonished to discover that a fellow immigrant of good repute and of humble station in the old world has, in the new world, acquired a past of remarkable grandeur—ancestral estates, titles, wealth, and close connections with those in high places. By the time the ship reaches the Statue of Liberty serious fractures of probity may already have occurred.

Probably there is no one who is not more liable to steal, to lie, or to commit adultery in a foreign land than at home. Some persons, indeed, travel for just this purpose—to lose an unwanted reinforcement of conscience. For them wanderlust is not a lust for wandering, but a wandering for lust—an effort to achieve abroad a license for which one could not forgive himself at home. Many persons do not need to go so far: the annual business convention in America is notorious in this respect. Things happen in motels that do not happen in homes, and towels are swiped in distant hotels by persons who would not steal a pin in their home towns. In these ways our increased mobility diminishes the external support for conscience.

Such support is withdrawn, also, by other changes. The rare person of today who does live out his life in the same town lives in a more heterogeneous culture than did his grandparents. The town has changed. Highways link it to the world; the products of faraway factories are for sale in its stores; in a thousand ways it has become connected with the larger society. The cultural horizons have receded; the diverse mores of distant cities seep in through each television antenna. Exposure to alien mores causes one to examine his native mores. And as soon as mores are examined they are seen to be relative;

their claim to absolute validity evaporates. The superego is thus deprived of that support that had been provided by the unquestioning acceptance of an unopposed pattern of life.

The increase of leisure operates to the same effect. Work strengthens conscience; leisure facilitates impulse. Idle hands are used by the devil. Work, therefore, has been considered a necessary aid to the superego in its task of curbing sexual and aggressive impulses. It is because of the strength of impulse that one must live by the sweat of his brow; painful labor is both punishment for past sin and insurance against further sinning. Work is best able to implement the control of impulse if it is difficult and continuous. On the one day of rest the church, with its reminder of guilt and original sin, is supposed to serve in lieu of work as adjuvant to conscience. To the extent that work has become easy and leisure has increased, the superego has been deprived of support in its function of repression.

Formerly God was regularly a part of the superego. Behind the authority of one's father was the greater authority of God; behind the towering figure of one's father loomed the vast image of the Father of us all. Both were incorporated by the child in the formation of the superego. The function of God within the superego was steadily aided by the continued existence of God in the outside world, in the same way that continued nearness to one's earthly father augmented the authority of the internalized father. The decline of religious belief has sharply diminished this support. Statistics of church membership are clearly no index to this decline. Belief in the supernatural propositions of religion has, beyond any doubt, radically diminished during the past fifty years. The extent of decline measures the loss of one of the most important external supports to the superego.

The following episode relates a crucial experience in superego formation. Though it occurred in this century, it portrays a relationship of father to son which was more characteristic of the nineteenth century. It seems, thereby, alien to our time, exaggerated in its harshness. Yet this is the way it happened.

GRASS

It was the last day of school. The report cards had been distributed, and—to his great relief—Larry found that he had passed. Now at eleven o'clock in the morning he was on his way home with two of his friends. They felt exhilaration at the prospect of three months of freedom and manifested it by pushing each other, yelling, throwing rocks at a bottle, chasing a grass snake, and rolling a log into the creek. Being nine years old, it took them a long time to reach their homes. Before parting they made plans to meet that afternoon to play ball. Larry ran through the tall grass up to the back door and into the kitchen. His mother was stirring something on the stove.

"Mama, I passed!"

"Not so loud, hon." She leaned over and kissed him, then looked at the report card. "This is very good. Show it to Daddy if he's not asleep."

He took the card and went through the bedroom to the porch. The bed faced away from the door and he could not tell whether his father were asleep or not.

"Daddy?"

"Come in, son."

"I passed," he said, offering the card.

Morris smiled and Larry averted his glance. He could never bring himself to face for long the level gaze of those gray eyes which seemed effortlessly to read his mind. His father looked over the report. "I see you got seventy-five in conduct."

"Yes, sir."

"Do you have an explanation?"

"No, sir."

"Do you think you deserved a better grade?"

"No . . . sir."

"Then you *do* have an explanation?"

Larry twisted one foot around the other. "Yes, sir. I guess so, sir."

"What is the explanation?"

This tireless interrogation could, Larry knew, be carried on for hours. Mumbling his words he began to recount his sins.

"I guess I . . . talked too much."

"Speak up, son."

"Yes, sir. I talked too much . . . and laughed . . . and cut up."

"Do you find silence so difficult?"

"Sir?"

"Was it so hard to be quiet?"

"Yes . . . sir. I guess so."

"You don't seem to find it difficult now."

He looked up and found his father smiling. It wasn't going to be so bad after all. "But the other grades are good," Morris said. Larry grinned and turned to look out the window. Heat waves shimmered above the tin roof of the barn, and away to the west was an unbroken field of sunflowers. Everything was bathed in, and seemed to be made drowsy by, the hot, bright sunlight. He thought of playing ball and wished dinner were over so that he could go now.

"Daddy, can I go over to Paul's house after dinner?"

Almost before the words were out he realized his mistake. He should have asked his mother first. She might have said yes without mentioning it to his father.

"No. You have to work, son."

"What've I got to do?"

Morris looked out over the several acres which were loosely referred to as the back yard. "You have to cut the grass."

Through a long wet spring the grass had sprung up until it was nearly a foot high. Now, in June, the rain was over and the heat was beginning to turn the grass brown. As the family had no lawn mower, any cutting of grass or weeds was done by hoe, scythe, or sickle. It was with one of these instruments that Larry assumed the grass would be cut, but he was mistaken. After dinner Morris gave him directions. The tool was to be an old, ivory-handled straight edge razor. The technique would be to grasp a handful of grass in the left hand and cut it level with the ground with the razor. The grass was to be put in a basket, along with any rocks or sticks that might be found on the ground. When the basket was full it was to be removed some hundred yards where the grass could be emptied and burned. When the razor was dull it was to be sharpened on a whetstone in the barn.

Larry changed his clothes, put on a straw hat, and went to work. Unable to realize the extent of the task or to gauge the time required, his only thought was to finish as soon as possible so as to be able to play before the afternoon were over. He began in the center of the yard and could see his father watching from the bed on the porch. After a few experimental slashes an idea occurred to him. He walked to the house and stood under the windows.

"Daddy."

"Yes, son."

"When I've finished can I play baseball?"

"Yes."

He resumed his work, thinking that he would cut fast and get it over in a couple of hours. For a few minutes the work went well, containing the satisfaction of watching the thin steel cut easily through dry grass. He grabbed big handfuls and hacked away with gusto. Soon his father called. Obediently he walked to the porch.

"Yes, sir?"

Morris was looking through a field glass at the small patch of ground that had been cleared.

"Son, I want you to cut the grass level with the ground. Therefore you will have to cut slower and more carefully. And it's better to hold a smaller handful because you can cut it more evenly. Also, you must pick up every stone." This referred to the few pebbles left in the cleared area. "Do you understand?"

"Yes, sir."

"Now go back and do that patch over again, and cut it even with the ground."

"Yes, sir."

Walking back he wondered why he had not started in some part of the yard out of his father's view. The work was now harder; for the stubble was only one or two inches high and was difficult to hold while being cut. It took an hour to do again the area originally cleared in a few minutes. By this time he was tired and disheartened. Sweat ran down his forehead and into his eyes, and his mouth was dry. The razor could not be held by the handle, for the blade would fold back. It had to be held by its narrow shank which already had raised a blister. Presently he heard his friends, and soon they came into view and approached the fence.

"Whatya doin'?"

"Cuttin' the grass."

"What's that you're cuttin' it with?"

"A razor."

They laughed. "That's a funny thing to be cuttin' grass with."

"Larry!" The boys stopped laughing and Larry went to the porch.

"Yes, sir?"

"If you want to talk to your friends, you may; but don't stop working while you talk."

"Yes, sir." He went back to the basket and resumed cutting.

"What'd he say?" Paul asked in a lowered voice.

"He said I had to work."

"You cain't play ball?"

"No."

"How long is he going to make you work?"

"I don't know."

"Well . . . I guess we might as well go on."

Larry looked up with longing. They were standing outside the fence, poking their toes idly through the palings. James was rhythmically pounding his fist into the socket of a first baseman's mitt.

"Yeah, let's get goin'."

"Can you get away later on?" Paul asked.

"Maybe I can. I'll try. I'll see if he'll let me." The two boys began to wander off. "I'll try to come later," he called urgently, hoping his father would not hear.

When they were gone he tried for a while to cut faster, but his hand hurt. Several times he had struck rocks with the razor, and the blade was getting dull. Gingerly he got up from his sore knees, went to the hydrant, allowed the water to run until cool, and drank from his cupped hands. Then he went to the barn and began whetting the blade on the stone. When it was sharp he sat down to rest. Being out of his father's sight he felt relatively secure for the moment. The chinaberry tree cast a liquid pattern of sun and shadow before the door. The berries were green and firm, just right for a slingshot.

"Larry!"

With a sense of guilt he hurried to his father's window. "Yes, sir."

"Get back to work. It's not time to rest yet."

At midafternoon he looked about and saw how little he had done. The heat waves shimmered before his eyes as he realized that he would not finish today and perhaps not tomorrow. Leaving the razor on the ground, he made the familiar trek to his father's window.

"Daddy."

"Yes."

"Can I quit now?"

"No, son."

"I cain't finish it this afternoon."

"I know."

"Then cain't I go play ball now and finish it tomorrow?"

"No."

"When can I play ball?"

"When you have finished cutting the grass."

"How long do you think it'll take me?"

"Two or three months."

"Well, can . . . ?"

"Now that's enough. Go back to work."

He resumed the work at a sullenly slow pace. To spare his knees he sat down, cutting around him as far as he could reach, then moving to a new place and sitting down again.

"Larry!"

He went back to the porch. "Yes, sir."

"Do you want to be a lazy, no-account scoundrel?" The voice was harsh and angry.

"No, sir."

"Then don't you ever let me see you sitting down to work again! Now you get back there as quick as you can and stand on your knees."

The afternoon wore on with excruciating slowness. The sun gradually declined. The thin shank of the razor cut into his hand and the blisters broke. He showed them to his father, hoping they would prove incapacitating, but Morris bandaged

them and sent him back. Near sundown he heard the sounds
of his friends returning home, but they did not come by to
talk. Finally his mother came to the back door and said that
supper was ready. The day's work was over.

When he awoke the next morning he thought it was another
school day. Then he remembered the preceding afternoon
and felt that school was not nearly as bad as cutting grass. He
knew that his father intended for him to continue the work,
but as no specific order had been given for this particular day
there was possibility of escape. He decided to ask his mother
for permission to play, and be gone before his father realized
what had happened. His mother was cooking breakfast when
he finished dressing. He made himself useful and waited until,
for some reason, she went on the back porch. Now they were
separated from his father by four rooms and clearly out of
earshot.

"Mama, can I go over to Paul's house?"

"Why yes, hon, I guess so."

That was his mother. To the reasonable request she said yes
immediately; the unreasonable required a varying amount of
cajolery, but in the end that, too, would be granted. When
breakfast was over, he quickly got his cap, whispered a soft
good-bye, and started out. He had reached the back door
when she called. "Be sure you come back before dinner."

"Larry!"

He stopped short. In another minute he would have been
far enough away to pretend he had not heard. But though his
conscience might be deaf to a small voice, it was not deaf to

this sternly audible one. If he ran now he would never be able to look at his father and say, "No, I didn't hear you." He gave his mother a reproachful glance as he went back through the kitchen. "Now I won't get to go," he said darkly.

He entered the porch and stood by the bed, his eyes lowered. He was conscious of omitting the usual verbal obeisance of "Yes, sir," but did not care.

"Where were you off to?"

"To Paul's."

"Who told you you could go?"

"Mama."

"Did you ask her?"

"Yes."

"Yes *what?*"

"Yes, sir," he said sulkily.

"Didn't you know I wanted you to work today?"

"No, sir."

"Don't you remember my telling you that you could not play until you finished cutting the grass?"

"No, sir." One lie followed another now. "Anyway . . . that will take just about . . . all summer." His mouth was dry and he was swallowing heavily. "James and Paul . . . don't have to work and . . . I don't see why . . . I . . . have to work all the time."

He flushed, his eyes smarted, and tears were just one harsh word away. After a moment of silence he saw the covers of the bed move. His father's long, wasted legs appeared. The tears broke, flooding his face. Morris stood up, found his slippers, and put on a bathrobe. Larry's ear was grasped and twisted by a bony hand, and he was propelled into the bathroom. Morris sat on the edge of the tub and held Larry in front of him. The fingers were relentless, and it seemed that the ear would be torn from his head.

"Look at me, son."

Tears were dripping from his chin, and every other moment his chest was convulsed by a rattling inspiration. Trying to stop crying, he managed at last to raise his head and look in his father's face. The head and neck were thin. The skin had a grayish glint, and the lines that ran down from his nose were straight. His eyes were steady, and on their level, searching gaze Larry's conscience was impaled.

"Do you know why you are going to be punished?"

The pose of injured innocence was gone now. His guilt seemed everywhere, and there was no place to hide.

"Yes . . . sir."

"Why?"

"Because . . . I . . . didn't tell the . . . truth." It was agony to look into those eyes.

"And?" The question was clipped and hard.

"And . . . because . . . ."

He tried to search his conscience and enumerate his sins, but his mind was a shambles and his past was mountainous with guilt. He could not speak. His eyes dropped.

"Look at me, son."

Painfully the wet eyes were again lifted to the steady gray ones above.

"You are being punished because you tried to get your mother's permission for an act you knew to be wrong. You were scoundrel enough to do that!" the knifelike voice said. "Do you understand?"

"Yes . . . sir."

"You are being punished, further, because you spoke in an ugly, sulky manner. Do you understand?"

"Yes . . . sir."

He saw the other hand move and felt the old, sick terror. The hand grasped the clothes of his back and lifted him onto his father's knees. His head hung down almost to the floor. The hand began to rise and fall.

"Do you understand why you're being punished?"

"Ye . . . es . . . sir."

The blows were heavy and he cried loudly.

"Will you ever do any of those things again?"

"No . . . sir."

The whipping lasted about a minute, after which he was placed on his feet. "Now, stop crying and wash your face. Then go out in the yard to work."

Still sobbing, he approached the lavatory and turned on a trickle of water. Behind him he heard his father stand and slowly leave the room. He held both hands under the faucet and with unseeing eyes stared at the drops of water tumbling over his fingers. Gradually the sobs diminished and presently ceased. He washed his face and left the room, closing the door softly. Passing through the kitchen he was aware that his mother was looking at him with compassion, but he avoided her eyes. To look at her now would be to cry again.

All that day he worked steadily and quietly. He asked no questions and made no requests. The work was an expiation and Morris found no occasion to criticize. Several times his mother brought out something cold for him to drink. She did not mention his punishment but knowledge of it was eloquent in her eyes. In the afternoon he began to feel better and thought of his friends and of playing ball. Knowing it to be out of the question for him, he merely dreamed about it.

That evening when supper was over and the dishes washed Morris called him.

"Tell him you're sorry," his mother whispered.

In their house after every punishment there must be a reconciliation. The integrity of the bonds that held them must be reaffirmed. Words of understanding must be spoken, tokens of love given and received. He walked out on the porch. The sky was filled with masses of purple and red.

"Do you feel better now, son?"

"Yes, sir." The gray eyes contained a reflection of the sunset. "I'm sorry I acted the way I did this morning."

A hand was laid on his head. "You said you didn't know why you had to work, didn't you?"

"Yes, sir, but I . . . ."

"That's all right, son. I'll tell you. You ought to know. When you are grown you will have to work to make a living. All your life you'll have to work. Even if we were rich you would labor, because idleness is sinful. The Bible tells us that. I hope some day you will be able to work with your head, but first you've got to work with your hands." The color of the ponderous clouds was deepening to blue and black. "No one is born knowing how to work. It is something we have to learn. You've got to learn to set your mind to a job and keep at it, no matter how hard it is or how long it takes or how much you dislike it. If you don't learn that you'll never amount to anything. And this is the time to learn it. Now do you know why you have to cut the grass?"

"Yes, sir."

"I don't like to make you work when you want to play, but it's for your own good. Can you understand that?"

"Yes, sir."

"Will you be a good boy and work hard this summer until the job is done?"

"Yes, sir."

He left the room feeling better. It was good to be forgiven, to be on good terms with one's father.

Day after day he worked in the yard, standing on his knees, cutting the grass close to the ground. There were few interruptions to break the monotony. Three or four times a day he went to the barn and sharpened the razor, but these trips were no escape. If he went too often or stayed too long his father took notice and put a stop to it. Many times each day he carried away the full basket of grass and stones, but the times of his departure and return were always observed. No evasions were possible because nothing escaped his father's eyes.

One day in July, at noon, he heard the rattle of dishes indicating that the table was being set. He was hot and tired and thirsty. He could almost smell the dinner cooking and thought of the tall glasses of iced tea. His mother came to the back door. At first he thought it was to call him, but she only threw out dishwater. Suddenly he dropped his razor and ran to the back steps.

"Mama," he called eagerly, but not loud enough for his father to hear. "Is dinner ready?"

"Yes, hon."

He came in, washed his hands, and sat in the kitchen to wait.

"Larry!"

It was his father's voice, the everlasting surveillance which he could not escape.

"Yes, sir."

"What did you come in for?"

"Mama said dinner was ready."

"Did you *ask* her?"

"Yes, sir."

"You trifling scoundrel! Get on back outside to work! And wait till she *calls* you to dinner! You understand?"

As weeks passed the heat increased and the grass withered. Had a match been touched to it the work of a summer would have been accomplished in a few minutes. No rain fell, even for a day, to interrupt the work. The grass did not grow, and the ground which was cleared on the first day remained bare. The earth was baked to a depth of four or five feet and began to crack. The only living thing he encountered was an occasional spider climbing desperately in or out of the crevices in search of a more habitable place to live. His friends knew he had to work and no longer came looking for him. Occasionally he would hear them playing in a nearby field, and sometimes in the mornings would see them pass with fishing poles over their shoulders. He knew that he was not missed, that they had stopped thinking of him and probably did not mention his name.

He became inured to the work but not reconciled to it, and throughout the summer continued to resist. Whippings—which had been rare before—were now common, and after each he would, in the evening, be required to apologize. He would go out on his father's porch, say he was sorry, and then listen guiltily to a restatement of the principles involved. Tirelessly Morris would explain what he had done wrong, the importance of learning to work, and the benefit to his character which this discipline would eventually bring about. After each of these sessions Larry would feel that he was innately shiftless, lazy, and impulsive. Each time he would resolve to try harder, but each time would relapse. After two or three days he would again become sullen or rebellious and again would be punished. Sometimes he saw his mother in tears and he knew that often she interceded in his behalf, but her efforts were ineffective.

Throughout June and July he worked every day except Sundays. As the job seemed endless he made no future plans. Anything that was apt to last all summer was too large an obstacle to plan beyond, any happiness that lay at its end too remote for practical anticipation. About the middle of August, however, his outlook changed. One evening at sundown he noticed that relatively little grass remained standing. For the first time since the beginning of summer he realized that his job would have an end and that he would soon be free. Surveying the area remaining to be cut, he attempted to divide it by the area which could be cleared in a single day and reached an estimate of five days. He felt a resurgence of hope and began visualizing what he would do when he was through. During the next several days he worked faster and more willingly, but found that he had been too sanguine in his estimate. He did not finish on the fifth day or the sixth. But on the evening of the seventh it was apparent to Morris as well as to him that the next day the job would be done. Only one or two hours of work remained.

The following morning—for the first time since May—he woke to the sound of rain. He wanted to work anyway, but was told that he could not. Then he asked if he could go to Paul's house to play until the rain stopped. Again the answer was no. About nine o'clock the rain let up and he hurriedly began to work. But the lull proved to be temporary and after a few minutes he had to stop. He stood under the awning which extended out over the windows of his father's porch and waited. After a while he sat on the ground and leaned against the house. A half hour passed. The rain was steady now, and seemingly would last all day. It dripped continuously from the canvas and formed a little trench in the earth in front of his feet. He stared out at the gray sky with a faraway, unseeing expression.

"I wish I could go to Paul's house."

He spoke in a low, sullen voice, hardly knowing whether he were talking to himself or to his father.

"It's not fair not to let me play . . . just because it's raining. It's not fair at all."

There was no comment from above. Minutes passed.

"You're a mean bastard!"

It seemed strange to be profane. He had never cursed before and was not at ease in the use of such words. Now, however, something violent was stirring in him, something that had been long stifled and was rankling for expression.

"If you think you can kick me around all the time you're wrong . . . you damned old bastard!"

At any moment he expected to be called. He would go inside and receive a whipping worse than he had thought possible. A long minute passed in silence.

Could it be that his father had not heard? That seemed unlikely, for often he had spoken from this place and been understood. The windows were open. There was nothing to prevent his hearing. Oh he had heard, all right. He was sure of that. Still, why wasn't he called? The waiting began to get on his nerves. Feeling that he could not make matters worse, he continued. This time he spoke louder and more viciously.

"You're the meanest man in the world. You lie up there in bed and are mean to everybody. I hate you!"

He began to feel astonished at himself. How incredible that he should be saying such things—he who had never dared a word of disrespect!

But why didn't his father call? What was he waiting for? Was he waiting for him to say his worst so as to be able to whip him all the harder? The rain drizzled down. The day was gray and quiet. The incident began to seem unreal. The absence of reaction was as incredible as the defamation. Both seemed impossible. It was like a bad dream.

But it's real! he thought furiously. He *had* said those things, and would keep on saying them till he made him answer. He became frantic and poured forth a tirade of abuse, a voluble, repetitious improvisation of profanity. He searched his memory for every dirty word he had heard, and when his store of obscene expletives was exhausted and he stopped, breathless, to listen . . . there was no response.

"You God damn dirty son of a bitch!" he screamed, "I wish you were dead! I wish you were dead, do you hear? Do you hear me?"

He had finished. Now something would happen. He cowered and waited for it, but there was no word from the porch. Not a sound. Not even the stir of bedclothes.

His rage passed and he became miserable. He sat with arms locked around his knees, staring blankly at the indifferent rain. As the minutes passed he became more appalled by what he had done. Its meaning broadened, expanded in endless ramifications, became boundless and unforgivable. He had broken the commandment to honor thy father and mother. He had taken the name of the Lord in vain, and that was the same as cursing God. He thought of his mother. What would she say when she learned? He pictured her face. She would cry.

For another half hour he sat there. He no longer expected to be called. For some reason the matter was to be left in abeyance. Finally, unable to endure further waiting, he got up and walked away. He went to the barn and wandered about morosely, expecting momentarily to see his mother enter to say that his father wanted him. But she did not come, and the morning passed without further incident.

On entering the house for lunch his first concern was to learn whether she knew. When she smiled he knew that she did not. Now that he was indoors he felt sure something would happen. He stayed as far from the porch as possible and spoke in low tones. Yet his father must know him to be present. He could not eat, and soon left the house and went back to the barn, where he felt somewhat less vulnerable.

He spent the afternoon there alone, sitting on a box, waiting. Occasionally he would get up and walk around aimlessly. Sometimes he would stand in the doorway looking out at the rain. Though unrestrained he felt himself a prisoner. He searched through his small understanding of his father but found no explanation of the delay. It was unlike him to postpone a whipping. Then it occurred to him that his act might have so far exceeded ordinary transgressions that it would require a special punishment. Perhaps he would not be whipped at all but would be sent away.

When supper time came he sneaked into the house and tried to be inconspicuous. His appearance was so haggard and agitated that his mother was concerned. She looked at him inquiringly and ran her hand affectionately through his hair. "What's the matter, son? Don't you feel well?"

"I feel all right," he said.

He escaped her and sat alone on the back porch until called to the table. When supper was safely over his situation was unimproved. It was too late to go outside again, and he could not long remain in the house without meeting his father. At the latest it could be put off only till family prayer. Perhaps that was the time when his crime would be related. Maybe they would pray for him and then expel him from home. He had just begun drying the dishes when the long awaited sound was heard.

"Larry."

It was not the wrathful voice he had expected. It was calm, just loud enough to be audible. Nevertheless it was enough to make him tremble and almost drop a plate. For a moment it seemed that he could not move.

"Your daddy wants you, dear."

He put down the dishtowel and went to the door of the porch.

"Yes, sir."

"Come out here where I can see you."

He approached the bed. His hands were clenched and he was biting his lip, trying not to cry.

"Your mother tells me you haven't been eating well today. You aren't sick, are you?"

"No, sir."

"You feel all right?"

"Yes, sir."

"Sit down, son. I just called you out here to talk for a while. I often think we don't talk to each other enough. I guess that's my fault. We'll have to do better in the future. I'd like to hear more about what you're interested in and what you think, because that's the only way I can get to know you." He paused a moment. "Maybe you think because I'm grown up I understand everything, but that's not true. You'll find as you get older that no matter how much you learn there's always much you don't know. For example you're my own son and I ought to know you pretty well, but every now and then something'll happen that'll make me realize I don't understand you at all."

Larry choked back a sob and tried to brace himself for the coming blow.

"I don't think I ever understood my father," Morris went on presently, "until it was too late. We were very poor—much poorer, son, than you can imagine. From year in to year out we might see only a few dollars in our house, and what little there was had to be spent for essentials. When we sold our cotton we'd have to buy a plow or an ax. And there were staple foods we had to buy like flour and sugar. We bought cloth, too, but never any ready-made clothes. Until I was a grown man I never had any clothes except what my mother made. I got my first store-bought suit to go away to medical school in, and I don't believe my mother ever had a store-bought dress. My father worked hard and made his boys work hard. We resented it and sometimes even hated him for it, but in the end we knew he was right. One of my brothers never could get along with Daddy, and he ran away from home when he was about fifteen. He turned out to be a no-account scoundrel, and the last I heard of him he was a saloon keeper in New Orleans.

"In the summer we hoed corn and picked cotton, and in the winter we fixed rail fences and chopped wood and hauled it home. And we always had mules and pigs to take care of. It was a very different life from yours . . . and in some ways a better one." He looked at Larry affectionately. "At any rate, we learned how to work, and there's nothing more important for a boy to learn. It's something you haven't yet learned, son. Isn't that right?"

"Yes, sir."

"You will, though. If you ever amount to anything you'll learn. You're learning now. I wish you could understand that

I wouldn't be trying to teach you so fast if I knew I would live long enough to teach you more slowly." He paused a moment. "Do you have anything to say?"

"No, sir."

"Then I guess you'd better see if your mother needs you."

Larry stood up, hardly able to believe that this was all.

"Son."

"Yes, sir."

"Come here a minute."

He went to the bed and his father put a hand on his shoulder. "Remember, son," he said in a husky voice, "whenever it seems I'm being hard on you . . . it's because I love you."

Late that night Larry woke frightened from a nightmare. For several minutes he lay in bed trembling, unable to convince himself that the vision was unreal. Presently he got up and tiptoed through the dark house to the porch.

"Daddy?" he whispered. "Daddy . . . are you all right?"

There was no reply, but soon he became aware of his father's regular breathing. He returned to bed but almost immediately got up and knelt on the floor.

"Dear God, please don't let anything happen to Daddy. Amen."

Still he could not sleep. He lay in bed and thought of many things, and after a while began worrying about the razor. What had he done with it? Was it still on the ground under the awning? Perhaps he had left it open. If so, someone might accidentally get cut. He got up again and went outside looking for it. In the dark he felt about on the ground under his father's windows but did not find it. Then he went to the barn and found it in its usual place and properly closed.

The following morning shortly before noon he completed his job. The last blade of grass was cut and carried away and the back yard was as bald as a razor could make it.

"Daddy," he said, standing under the porch window, "I've finished. Is it all right?"

Morris looked over the yard, then took his binoculars and scrutinized it in more detail, particularly the corners.

"That's well done, son."

Larry put away the basket and razor and came inside. After dinner he began to feel uncomfortable. It seemed strange not to be working. Restless and unable to sit still, he wandered about the house, looking out the windows and wondering what to do. Presently he sought and obtained permission to go to Paul's house, but he felt he was doing something wrong.

During the next two weeks he often played with his friends but never fully lost himself in play and was secretly glad when school started and life settled down to a routine again. He was more quiet than before and better behaved, and when next the report cards were distributed he had a nearly perfect score in conduct.

THE DIMINISHED UNCONSCIOUS

The discipline imposed on Larry was intensely personal, and the superego it created was likewise personal. It was indelibly drawn, and it wore the very image of his father's face. In these days the superego has become depersonalized.[5] It is no longer so predominantly the father who organizes life and value for the son; for the authority of the father has diminished. Culture contemporary to the child now plays a larger part; and since culture now presents diverse and conflicting mores, the super-ego that results is less well integrated and wields diminished authority. It is thereby less effective as a carrier of tradition. We do not escape the past altogether; but in the superego of the man of today the image of parents is fainter, their lifespan shorter.

With the decline of the superego, morality has changed in content. Many things at which our grandparents would have drawn the line now pass muster; and we balk at some things which caused them no compunction. But, apart from changes in the content of moral behavior, there have been changes in the source of morality, the mode of conformity to moral directives, and the site of moral authority.

Formerly morality was obedience to the verities instilled by parents; it is coming now to be compliance with the prac-tices of one's peers.[6] In both instances the source of the stand-ard is outside the individual; for moral principles, not being innate, must be somewhere acquired. In the nineteenth century they were learned from the older generation; now they are learned largely from contemporaries. This shift in source of moral directives is clearly a function of the accelerating rate of social change; for if social change of such magnitude as to require adaptive characterological change is occurring rapidly, the cues will be given first by one's contemporaries.

The change in conformity is less obvious. It is not that now one conforms to the group whereas formerly one went his own way. Conformity is common to both modes: formerly one conformed to the precepts of parents; now one conforms to the expectations of contemporaries. Yet there is a difference in the style of conformity. When the source of morality is in the past one is more likely to abstract principles; when the source is in the present one is more likely to ape models. The change detracts from the reflective and judicial quality of moral action, discourages the examination of a unique situation with reference to a guiding principle, and fosters the adoption of total behavioral modes. This gives to morality an automaton quality. It tends, indeed, to make morality synonymous with adjustment.

The site of the moral standard has also changed. The group has gained in authority at the expense of the conscience. Formerly the standard whereby conduct was judged was within the individual. It was taken from the older generation, but the point is that it was *taken*. It was incorporated by the individual in his childhood and thereafter endured within him, beholden to no one, paying no tribute. Now the standard whereby conduct is judged is coming to be located in the group to which the individual adjusts. Specifically this means that the superego has become weaker, more susceptible to influence. The grounds on which it praises and prohibits are open to argument and, particularly, to example.

Consequent to the diminished authority of the superego, unconscious motivation has become less significant in human affairs—for the reason, simply, that there now is less of it. As the authority and stability of the superego have diminished, it has become less able to exclude psychic elements from consciousness. Therefore, there has occurred in society as a whole during the past two generations a development analogous to that which occurs in an individual during psychoanalysis, an expansion of awareness at the expense of the unconscious.

The contraction of the unconscious is empirical: it may be observed. Many elements of motivation which were commonly repressed in the nineteenth century are now rarely repressed. The evidence concerning aggression is equivocal, but there is no doubt about the liberation of sexuality. The diminished incidence of hysteria is in line with these observations, and is similarly a matter of fact. Hysteria depends upon repression, and is becoming rare; character disorders reflect warped ego-functioning, and are becoming common. As clear-cut symptom neuroses disappear, vague conditions of aimlessness and futility become prevalent.

The contraction of the unconscious may also be theoretically derived from known cultural changes. For the superego, which is the instrument of repression, is the internal representative of the culture. As the culture changes, the superego necessarily changes; and as the superego changes, a change in the unconscious is to be expected. The superego does not, however, represent all aspects of culture; it is the representative only of those aspects of culture which have here been designated as the institutional process. The instrumental process develops at an accelerating pace, and the institutional process gives ground. The superego, being a precipitate of institutional verities, likewise gives ground. The contraction of the unconscious may thus be inferred from this reciprocal development.

In addition to the quantitative change in the unconscious, there has occurred also a qualitative change. Formerly the superego was the primary source of repression; now the ego is more commonly the agency that excludes perceptions and motivations from awareness. In the nineteenth century, man lived in a society of relatively stable values. These were transmitted to him by his parents and established within his character as a relatively permanent and autonomous agency. A drive conflicting with this agency was repressed. If sufficiently strong, this drive achieved a distorted symptomatic discharge which constituted the illness. Neurotic suffering in the present is coming more and more to derive from a quite different process. Society does not embody such generally accepted patterns of value, and the individual is caught in a dilemma: if out of the multitudinous choices of modern life he commits himself to certain values and with them builds a durable identity, he is apt to lose contact with a rapidly changing world; if he does not commit himself, but maintains an alert readiness to move with the current, he suffers a loss of the sense of self. Not knowing what he stands for, he does not know who he is. This occasions the anxiety which is coming to be the name of our age. Any development that threatens further to liquefy this already fluid sense of identity may increase anxiety to an unendurable pitch and hence prompt the ego to exclude the threatening wish or perception from awareness.

In the nineteenth century the unconscious consisted largely

of superego rejects. Being the polar opposite of a known quantity, it was more homogeneous, more subject to inference. Nowadays the unconscious is comprised largely of ego rejects and is heterogeneous. In it sexual wishes, certainly, have lost their former pre-eminence. Being the product of the anxiety suffered by a fluid identity, it is the polar opposite of nothing definite.

RETREAT FROM REASON

In the eighteenth century, having discarded the world view which had for centuries been imposed by the Church, man achieved by reason a blueprint of the universe. The great plan was seen in outline; it remained only to fill in the details. The universe was a precision instrument, a great clock that, having been set in motion, would continue forever. It functioned, not at the whim of God, but according to its own law. However cleverly hidden its secrets, they would all yield in time to the probing reason of enlightened man. Goodness, order, and uniformity were built into the nature of things. Progress would consist in approximating human nature and institutions to natural law.

Now there is no great plan or pattern. The blueprint has been lost. Nothing is static. Everything evolves. We speak less of progress than of survival; and survival may be had only by adapting human nature and institutions to existing conditions of human life. The existing conditions undergo change at an accelerated rate, and seldom can a present problem be solved by a formula from the past.

From the eighteenth century until our own time it had

seemed that reason could establish values of demonstrable validity, not only for the culture in which they arose, but for all peoples. In our time this position is being replaced by a cultural nihilism which reduces value to taste. It had seemed that precise science yielded absolute truth and that there was no limit to the penetrability of matter by science. Now the causal law is being replaced by the probability law, and our vision of the microcosmic world is limited in theory as well as practice. The currency of the phrase "indeterminacy principle" measures the appeal of its words rather than an understanding of the hypothesis, and the frequent allusions to this principle by social scientists bespeak an incipient readiness to give up the whole notion of a determined universe. The idea of progress has fallen into bad repute. It had seemed that technological progress would achieve progressive betterment of the human condition; now it is more common to regard the machine as the unruly and malevolent master of man. The atomic bomb and the assembly line are the present fruits of technology, and to many it appears a toss-up whether we shall die by blast or boredom. It had seemed that psychoanalysis would extend the realm of reason to include the most obscure and devious elements of mental life. Now Freud is claimed by the opposite camp. His greatest achievement, so it is said, is that of having exposed reason as the shoddy tissue of rationalizations that it is, and he is credited with having fathered the cult of the irrational.

Having lost faith in absolute values, we have become skeptical, also, of instrumental values. In the storm of change, we have jettisoned not only the excess baggage, but also the crucially important ballast. The retreat from reason, having gotten underway in the twenties, has so gained in speed and momentum that it is coming now to be known as a revolt.[7] "Man, having found that he cannot live by reason alone, seems determined that he will not live by reason at all."

The retreat from reason is reactive to the troubles of our times. Two world wars, a world depression, dictatorships, purges, and the present possibility of winding the whole thing up on the next slip—all this is within the lifetime of living men. Surveying this state of affairs, many persons find an explanation which appears obvious: science has imposed a godless materialism on western civilization, destroying those values which had provided for the support and security of man. Science, it may be allowed, has its place, but is out of place when it impinges on traditional values and institutions. In times of trouble the past is transformed, becomes an age of innocence and clarity. The evil was ushered in by change. Technology is the instrument of change. Behind technology stands science, behind science the method of rational inquiry, and, finally, reason itself. So science and reason are blamed, together and alone, for the evils of our day. Reason has had two hundred years in which to prove its right to direct the course of human affairs, and has brought us to the verge of universal destruction.

Those who are committed to reason are quick to point out that the accusation is both unfair and inconsistent. The social disasters of the twentieth century have issued out of economic and political practices and the relations between nations, and it is from precisely these areas that scientific method has been most rigorously excluded. When the findings of disinterested inquiry have run counter to vested interests, rational inquiry has usually been thrown out. Moreover the period prior to the last two centuries was not lacking in brutal wars, in purges, plagues, and starvation.

But the rebuttal does not convince, and more and more of those who are troubled by the crisis of our times call for a rebirth, in one form or another, of transcendental values.

Although reactive to the troubles of our times, the retreat from reason is not explained by these troubles. Past times have encountered comparable problems without being forced to flight. The retreat from reason, like the changing social character, is an outcome of the quickened and still accelerating rate of cultural change which is rendering obsolete many of the great intellectual systems of the past. Reason does not lose value, but fixed embodiments of reason become outdated. The goals which have held the allegiance of men and which have been superannuated by change have not all been products of faith. Many of them have been products of reason, and most of them have retained the guise of reason even after they have come to function as dogma.

But whatever guise it may wear, dogma claims finality. In its own domain it holds that its word is the last word, and any challenge of that word is heresy. Sooner or later changing conditions force the abandonment of such positions; and where dogma wears the guise of reason the discrediting of dogma discredits reason. For reason is not judged on its own merits; the products of reason are constantly transformed by the quest for certainty into articles of faith. They function then as a call to emotion rather than to critical intelligence. Being petrified into dogma they become the exact opposite of the rational inquiry that engendered them. But having remained for true believers as symbols of reason, their final collapse is taken as a collapse of reason.

Marxism is an example of such a development. Many Americans of this century passed from religion to Marxism during their college years, experiencing this as a transition from faith to reason, from transcendental values to rational values, from a mythological cosmogony to a scientific interpretation of history. There was much to support such a view. Marx's analysis of capitalism was certainly an exercise of intelligence rather than faith; and the communist movement, so it seemed, was the direct outcome of that critical analysis. But although Marxism remained a symbol of rational inquiry, it ceased to be so in fact. It came indeed to be hostile to any disinterested review of the facts. It died as reason but lived as dogma, with its adherents remaining unaware of the change. When the developments of the last two decades forced the abandonment of the Marxian dream, many of the former dreamers felt that reason was bankrupt. It should occasion no surprise that ex-communists feel particularly drawn toward mysticism, Catholicism, and reactionary politics.

Institutional absolutes and the coercive power systems that

protect them have never provided real security; but they create a subjective feeling of security. The chains that enslave also guard one from the unknown. The uses of reason have cut away most of our immemorial myths and superstitions, and without them we cringe in the sharp winds of uncertainty. We feel lost without the old ceremonial guarantees, afraid to trust our own processes of intelligent inquiry, for these seem too fallible. We have fallen victim to our own power to destroy our myths. Now we so miss the security of our former shackles that we are inclined to discard the sharp-edged tool that cut them. If we do, we shall not have long to wait before someone fits us out with a new set.

Clearly it is not reason that has failed. What has failed—as it has always failed, in all of its thousand forms—is the attempt to achieve certainty, to reach an absolute, to bind the course of human events to a final end. Reason cannot serve such a purpose and yet remain reason. By its nature it must be free to perceive emergent problems and meet them with new solutions. It is not reason that has promised to eliminate risk in human undertakings; it is the emotional needs of men, fastening onto the products of reason, that have made such promises. The vision of a state of universal peace and happiness, to be achieved by reason, is quite transparently the same old heavenly city which was to have been reached by faith and repentance.[8] The reason of the Enlightenment was, as Carl Becker has shown, a new religion. Natural law became a synonym for divine providence; the regularity of the universe was equivalent to the goodness of God; and the pursuit of truth was the new guise for the search for salvation. When a religion is built with the products of science it functions as does any other religion: it erects absolute truth as a dyke against the encompassing tides of change, risk, and uncertainty. Eventually such dykes crumble. In our time of quickened and rising tides they crumble faster than ever.

ADAPTATION TO CHANGE

Truth is hard to get in a net of words: some part of it slips through, or else one gets so much else besides that one cannot see truth whole and uncluttered. The view of life as change and flow appears at variance with the tragic view which finds the essentials of man's condition to be unchanging. "The thing that hath been, it is that which shall be; and that which is done is that which shall be done: and there is no new thing under the sun." The awareness of mortality, and of yearnings that would reach beyond death—this has always been man's fate. Grief and greed, desire and hate—these remain the same. To be born, to work, to suffer, to have fleeting joys, to die—these do not change.

The light of eternity does not illumine the temporal; by definition it reflects only the eternal. In this essay life is viewed in the light of every day, a level of abstraction at which the data assume a temporal and changing aspect. These two views do not conflict, do not contend for the same truth. One need not, and cannot, choose between them. They formulate distinct levels of experience.

The continuity of acceleration in the rate of cultural change is the clue to the emergent social character. The character corresponds to the rate that has now been reached.

Now, for perhaps the first time in his life on earth, man is obliged to adjust, not simply to changed conditions, but to change itself. In the past he had to give up the old and adapt to the new; now he must adapt, also, to the certain knowledge that the new, with unprecedented rapidity, is being replaced by that which is to follow. Before he becomes fully acquainted with the emerging circumstances of life he is distracted by the moving shadows of their unknown successors. As a modern aircraft may be obsolete by the time it comes off the production line, so the conditions of man's life begin to pass away before he has fairly come to grips with them.

In the last century, to be sure, great changes were encompassed in a single lifetime. Our grandfathers were forced in adult life to adjust to conditions radically different from those of their childhood. Yet the duration of an apparently unchanged culture was greater then than now, and fewer characterological changes were required in a lifetime.

Nowadays no character that is fixed can remain adjusted— unless experience is limited to those conditions under the influence of which character was formed, in which event the dimensions of life shrink rapidly. To be of fixed character and also receptive to the environing culture generates a mounting tension—a circumstance in which psychiatrists become acquainted with a large number of their patients. To remain open to a changing culture and also adapted to it implies the capacity for characterological change. For there is no longer any such thing as an average predictable environment. The only thing that can be predicted with certainty is continued acceleration in the rate of cultural change.

GOOD-BYE, MAMA

Caroline and Larry sat on a bench in the waiting room of the railroad station in San Antonio. Caroline was wearing a black dress that fitted her badly. Her hair had turned completely white within a few months after the death of her husband nine years previously. She was now forty-five. During the past year she had been through a serious illness which had robbed her of the last appearance of youth and left her frightened and unable to act for herself. Her son had, with some difficulty, persuaded her to put her house in the hands of a real-estate agent, and go and stay with relatives. Larry was tall and thin, and just eighteen. He had with him a copy of Kant's *Critique of Pure Reason*, which he read with a quiet absorption that she tried not to break in upon.

At last, unable to keep still any longer, she asked, "What did we do with the living-room set?"

"Left it in the house," Larry murmured, without looking up from his book.

"Left it in the house?"

"You know that, Mother. We discussed it often enough," he said patiently.

"We shouldn't have left it," Caroline said. "That's not the right kind of furniture to leave in a rented house. It's solid walnut. Your daddy bought it for me at an auction. We should have put it in storage."

The station vibrated slightly to an arriving train. Larry looked at the clock and then across the waiting room at the bulletin board, where the incoming and outgoing trains were indicated in white chalk. There was still half an hour before the departure time of their trains, due to leave at almost the same moment, for different destinations. He tried to go on reading, found that he couldn't concentrate, and closed the book. His glance came to rest first on his own luggage, a single suitcase, and then on his mother's four suitcases, two of them shabby and dilapidated, with heavy cord tied around them to keep them from bursting open.

"Don't you want me to check those two old suitcases?" he asked.

She did not appear to hear him. Her lips moved, as if she were talking to herself.

"Mother," he said, touching her arm and then indicating the dilapidated suitcases. "I'd better check those two on your ticket."

"What's that?" she cried, her voice full of alarm. "What are you going to do?"

"I'm going to check your bags," he said, and stood up.

"No," she said. "Don't do that."

"You can't manage four by yourself," he said. "You have to change at Shreveport and Monroe. What if you can't find a redcap?"

"Hon," she said, brushing this problem aside, "where did we put that little baby dress of yours?"

He sighed and sat down. "I don't know. But it doesn't matter. It was falling apart anyway."

"Why, dear! I wouldn't part with that dress for the world.

It's pure silk. Your grandmother spent months making it—before you were born. Didn't you see the fine handwork on it?"

"Yes," he said wearily. "I saw it. Don't worry. It must be in one of the boxes we stored. It's bound to be there, because we didn't throw anything away—not even a thirty-year-old newspaper."

"I wish I could remember where my things were," Caroline said plaintively.

Nervous and withdrawn, she sat and clutched her purse. A gray-haired Negro, red cap in hand, planted himself in front of the bulletin board and in a long, rolling cadence announced the arrival and impending departure of the Sunset Limited. Suddenly, Caroline leaned forward and untied the cord around one of the old suitcases. In spite of her son's protests, she opened the suitcase and began going through the contents.

The bag was filled with fragments of the past, carefully folded and lovingly packed: surgical instruments that had belonged to Larry's father; a souvenir of Lookout Mountain; a wedding veil; baby shoes; a bullet mold that had been used by her son's great-grandfather; sheet music; bundles of ancient letters; a certificate of membership in the Woodmen of the World, dated 1905.

"Mother, you're absolutely hopeless!" Larry exclaimed. He had previously thrown away about half the contents of this bag as being of no value, and the rest he had put in a box for storage. His mother must have been up most of the preceding night retrieving and packing these things.

Since Caroline could never throw anything away, the closets and the attic had been piled high with old possessions, and the

process of sorting and packing had brought to light innumer-
able items evocative of the past. Though ostensibly engaged
in discarding the useless and packing the valuable, actually
she had done neither. She had merely gone through their
belongings one by one, fondled them, talked about them, and
cried now and then. At the end of a morning's work, she
would be surrounded by piles of souvenirs, from not one of
which was she willing to be separated. Larry, on the other
hand, had ransacked ruthlessly, and his mother had spent much
of her time recovering the things he threw away. The work
of one had neutralized that of the other. Sometimes they had
both been in one of the large closets together, he on a step-
ladder plowing through the piles of miscellany on the top
shelf. "We don't want this any more," he would say, tossing
something down on the floor. "Or this. Or this." And she, as
these reminders of the past fell around her, would stoop and
pick each one up, smooth it out, and place it lovingly among
the things she wanted to keep.

"What in the world do you want with this?" he asked now
as he leaned over and took out a little brown bottle that he
remembered throwing in the trash basket several days before. Caroline took it from him. "Why, hon, this medicine
once saved your life. You fell down a long flight of stone
steps when you were just three years old. That was when we
were up in Chattanooga, and your daddy said that if it hadn't
been for this medicine, you would've died."

"What is it?" Larry asked.

"I don't know. I think it's adrenalin."

"Well, it's no good now!"

"I know, but I think we ought to keep it," Caroline said.
"What for?"

"Well, it saved your life," she said, putting the bottle back in the suitcase. "We don't want to throw away any of our keepsakes."

She resumed her search, lifting sections of the contents of the suitcase here and there and peering in at the deeper layers. Presently, she said something under her breath and began untying the other old suitcase. It was filled with a similar assortment of souvenirs. She looked through it, without finding what she was looking for. Then she sat up straight. "Hon, where did we put that picture of your daddy?"

"Which one?" Larry asked.

"The big one in the gold frame. You know—the one on the wall over the piano."

"We left it there."

"*Left* it there?" Caroline repeated incredulously.

"You can have the agent mail it to you if you want it," he said.

For a moment Caroline sat quite still. Then a stubborn expression came over her face, and hurriedly she tied up the two suitcases. When she had finished, she got up and walked away. Her son called to her. She stopped, came back, and picked up one of her suitcases. Larry went over to her and caught her arm. "Mama, what's the matter?" he asked. "What are you doing?"

"Well, now, son, sit down and I'll tell you," Caroline said. "I'll tell you what I've decided." She patted his hand as they sat down on the bench. "I've decided I won't go."

"You *can't* change your mind now!" he cried. "Everything's all set. We're about to get on the train."

"No, I've made up my mind," she said. "This is my home. All my things are here. I belong here."

"If *you* don't go, I can't go, either," Larry said.

"Yes, you can, too. I wouldn't hold you back. You go right ahead."

Larry looked at the clock and swallowed hard. "We've been through all this before," he said. "We've made the right decision. You've been very sick and . . . ."

"I know," Caroline said, "and I'll never forget what you did for me." She had refused to leave her home when she became sick. None of their relatives had been able to stay with her and see her through a prolonged illness. Helen was away in El Paso teaching school. There wasn't the money to engage a nurse. "I'd never have gotten well any place but here," she said, "and there was no one else could stay here with me. If you hadn't dropped out of school and come home and nursed me so well, I'd not be living now. I'd . . . ."

"That's not the point, Mama. Listen, please. Will you listen to what I say?"

"Yes, son."

"You're a lot better now, but still not entirely well. You need a long rest. You know what the doctor told you. And I ought to go back to college."

"Yes, I know you should, hon."

"But the point is that you're not well enough to stay here alone," Larry said.

"Why, yes, I am."

"There'd be no one to look after you if you got sick again. You wouldn't feed yourself properly," he said.

"Yes, I will."

"You didn't the last time you were left alone."

"I've learned my lesson now."

"Mama, don't let's argue about it. It's all settled."

"But this is my home," Caroline said. "What would I do in Leeville?"

"Grandma and Grandpa are there," Larry said. "Uncle Marshall and Aunt Minnie are there. You can rest. And there'll be people to look after you."

"I don't need anyone to look after me," Caroline said.

"Yes, you do," Larry said. "I'm going to be away at school all winter, and probably all next summer. What's the sense in your staying here alone? You have no relatives near here. You'd be lonesome. You'd have to cook for just yourself, and keep up a big house, and you wouldn't have anybody to talk to, or take care of you if you got sick. I just don't like to think of it."

"You and Helen will be coming home for your vacations," Caroline said.

"It's not worth it, keeping the house just for that," he said.

"You mustn't worry about me, son. I've been looking after myself for a long time, and I certainly ought to know how by now," Caroline said.

He slumped dejectedly. "All right, then," he said. "If you stay, I stay. I can't leave you alone."

"No, hon, that's . . . ."

"I'm not going to discuss it any more," he said irritably.

"I'm sick of it. We've been round and round this business for weeks. Every time I think it's settled, you change your mind. Then we go through the same old thing all over again. Now I'm through talking about it. If you won't go, then I have to stay and look after you—at least until I can find someone else to do it."

A man sat down across from them, stared at them, and then began to read a paper. Larry scuffed the sole of one shoe against the other.

"All right, son," his mother said, finally. "I'll go."

For several moments they sat in silence. Then Caroline said, more to herself than to her son, "I think I saw the photograph album just now in one of those bags."

Again she untied one of the old suitcases.

"You're going to wear those things out opening and closing them," he said to her. "Why don't you let me check them?"

Caroline found the photograph album and for a few minutes seemed relatively at peace as she turned its pages.

"Look, dear," she said, taking hold of her son's arm. "Do you know who that pretty little baby is?"

"No," he said, "but from the tone of your voice I gather it's me."

"Yes, it is," Caroline said, and lapsed into a sort of baby talk. "You were just the cutest, preciousest little baby there ever was. That's what you were!"

Gently disentangling himself from her grasp, he said, "You'd better let me close up this bag now." When he had retied the suitcase, he found her looking at a small, faded oval photograph. "Who's that?" he asked.

"A picture of your daddy as a boy. See the date on it? It was taken in Monroe, in 1893."

Caroline began to cry. "How can I go?" she asked. "All my things are in my house. There's no other place to put them. Nobody else will ever take care of them—you know that. It'll never be the same after other people live there. They'll bang things up, be careless and destructful of the things we love!"

People were looking at her curiously, and her son was embarrassed.

"Don't feel so bad about it, Mama," he said in a low voice, putting an arm around her. "Of course there'll be some wear and tear, but you'll be getting rent. Maybe when you come back, you'll have enough money saved to fix the house up like you've always wanted to. Anyway, we're not leaving anything that's valuable."

The words had little meaning for her, but she drank in his kindness and seemed comforted.

"I don't know what I'd do without you, dear," she said. "You're always so good to me."

"You'll be all right."

"I know I will," she said.

"Now, try to relax, Mama. It's almost train time. Don't look through the bags any more. Nothing has been lost."

"All right, dear." She folded her hands in her lap, as if making an effort to compose herself. Once, she leaned forward to do something with one of the suitcases, but caught herself and sat up straight again. "You know, hon," she said presently, "we won't go on to Leeville tonight. We're both tired. When we get to Shreveport, we'll go to a hotel and get a good night's sleep."

Larry felt a cold hand at his heart. "Mother. You know, don't you, that I'm not going with you?"

"Where are you going?" Caroline asked.

"Mother! Pull yourself together, *please!* You know I'm going to Baton Rouge—to school."

"Oh, yes—yes."

He looked away and took a deep breath, feeling a mounting anxiety. He looked at the clock. Another fifteen minutes to wait. He had an intense longing to have it over with.

She took one of his hands in hers. "I wish you could go to Leeville with me," she said. "After all, you need a vacation, too."

"Are you sure you won't let me check two of your bags?" he asked. "It'd be a lot easier for you."

"You do whatever you think best, dear."

"I have to have your ticket," he said.

She gave it to him, and he picked up the two old bags. She held his arm and looked at him as though she could not allow him out of sight. "I'll go with you," she said.

"No, Mother, please! You stay here with our other things. I'll be right back."

Reluctantly she sat down. He could feel her watching him as he crossed the station. After checking the bags, he stood around the baggage room for a few minutes.

"You know," she said as soon as he returned, "I've been

thinking—and I've got an idea that seems very good to me."

"What is it?"

"Why don't I go to Baton Rouge with you, instead of to Leeville? We could rent an apartment with what we get from our house here. We'd be together and could look after each other. I could make a home for you. I'd enjoy that."

"I don't think that's a good idea, Mother," he said.

"Why not, hon?"

"Things are too uncertain. I don't want you to have to do housework and shopping and cooking. You need a long rest. There are a lot of reasons."

"We could make out all right if we were together," Caroline said.

"No, I don't think it would be wise," Larry said.

"Don't you want me with you?"

"Of course, Mother. I'm just telling you what I think best for both of us."

"I know you are," she said quickly.

"Come on, Mama," he said, unable to wait any longer. "I think I heard them announce your train. Anyway, we should be able to get on now."

He picked up the three remaining bags, and they went down into the underpass and came up at Track 5, where her train was. The conductor waited beside the steps of the first coach. He stood aside for them to board the train. Caroline hesitated. Larry put his own suitcase on the platform and gently impelled her forward by pressure on her arm, but she held back.

"Go ahead, Mother."

She turned and caught the lapels of his coat, as though afraid of the train.

"Go ahead," he told her. "I'll get on with you."

This magically overcame her reluctance, and she climbed the steps. When they were seated on facing green plush seats, she leaned forward with a worried expression, as if she could no longer put off telling him something of the greatest importance; yet she said nothing. Unable to avoid her eyes indefinitely, he forced himself to look at her, and smiled. She caught his hand in both of hers, pressed it, caressed it, pleading mutely that he not go entirely away from her, that he save some part of his life and heart for her.

"Well," he said, "I guess it's about time to go."

She looked at him with eyes large and wet with tears. "Be a good boy, son," she said. "I know you will. Get plenty of sleep and don't work too hard."

As she obviously had not finished, he waited, but she seemed lost in thoughts of a different nature and did not continue.

The car was filling up. A woman with a baby sat down across the aisle from them. The baby was crying. A porter squeezed by their seats, carrying four handbags. A newsboy came down the aisle hawking the San Antonio *Express*, and made two sales.

"I really have to go now," Larry said. "This train is going to leave in a minute, and mine is, too. Well—good-bye, Mama."

He put his arms around her. Suddenly the thought of losing him seemed to strike her with new force; she held on to him and would not let go. He looked down on the white hair and felt agonizingly small. He loosened her arms gently and turned away. After a few steps down the aisle, he stopped and called to her. "Have you got your ticket?"

She was looking at him and did not understand. "What? What's that?"

"Your ticket?" he said.

"My ticket?"

The faint expression of annoyance that crossed his face seemed to make her comprehend. "Oh," she said. "Oh, yes. You gave it back to me."

For a moment more, his glance met hers. He tried to smile affectionately; then he turned and quickly left the car.

Passing her window on the outside, with his suitcase, he looked up and saw her eyes anxiously fixed on him through the glass. He smiled, waved, and went on. After about twenty feet, he stopped again, looked back, and found that she had turned around in her seat, so as to follow him with her eyes until the last possible moment. He threw her a kiss. She returned the gesture with clumsy haste, dropping her purse as she did so.

Larry descended the steps to the underpass, came up again at Track 6, and boarded the train that would take him to Baton Rouge. When he was seated, he glanced out the window and, to his surprise, found that he could still see his mother. Their trains were on adjacent tracks, and a distance of no more than fifteen feet separated the car he was sitting in from hers. He could see her clearly and, if it were not for the two layers of glass, could have spoken to her. She was still looking backward, in the direction in which he had gone. Her hands gripped her purse tightly. She was wearing the old black dress that had been her Sunday best for so many years. When she turned and settled in her seat, he thought surely she would see him. But almost immediately she looked back again, as if on the remote chance that he might reappear.

His train left first. As it began slowly to move, it must have created for her the illusion that her train was moving—for she looked back more urgently, twisting her body, straining for one more glimpse of him. In this attitude of yearning, loss, and farewell, she disappeared from his view.

V { PSYCHOANALYSIS
AND
IDENTITY

DOGMA AND PSYCHOANALYSIS

In the retreat from reason the position of psychoanalysis is ambiguous. As a psychology it has been applied fruitfully in many fields, being changed in the process. In this sense it participates in the continuing progress of knowledge and exerts an influence counter to the retreat from reason. As a therapeutic science, however, it surrounds itself with barriers and tends to become encapsulated. It still produces some open-minded inquiry, but there are indications that it may harden into dogma. In America it has nestled under the wing of the medical profession, becoming all but inaccessible to those who are not physicians. From this association it does not enrich itself as a science; it gains only as a guild. It secures for itself the institutional protection and prerogatives of medicine, but loses by the exclusion of those persons whose consistent interest in human nature has led them to the study of subjects more pertinent to this interest than those taught in medical schools. It thereby diminishes its contact and interaction with the related sciences of psychology, sociology, and anthropology. It moves toward the position of an absolute science, channeling its energy into the endeavor of filling in the remaining unknowns in a fixed system. Conjecture is likely to be accepted as fact if it fits the configuration of a lacuna. It seems to be entering a stage of scholasticism, becoming increasingly preoccupied with the abstruse, the minute, and the unverifiable. Along this path, if it continues, it will soon reach the question of how many cathexes can dance on the point of a projection.

Several factors force it along this path. One of these is historical, deriving from the way in which psychoanalysis was organized into a going concern.

Freud's work was quickly institutionalized, and thereafter was defended and promoted as a vested interest. The basic discoveries of psychoanalysis endowed a social movement. Those who deviated too far were expelled, among them many of the most gifted and creative. An analyst is still expected to identify himself as Freudian or non-Freudian. Though many of the early defenders of psychoanalysis were amateurs, most of the defensive and promotional work has been done by professionals. And when one holds stock in the institution one promotes, it becomes difficult to know for sure that the promotion proceeds only from love of truth.

This development has left its imprint on psychoanalysis. The likely effects are manifest in the contrasting developments of the discoveries of two other innovators of the same era, Marx and Darwin.

Marx, like Freud, used his work as the capital endowment of a social movement. Competing movements were systematically attacked. People were divided into Marxists and non-Marxists. Authorized interpreters were on hand to designate new ideas as valid or as counterrevolutionary. The interests of maintaining and strengthening the movement consistently took precedence over the further disinterested study of social conflict. By these means the creative product of Marx's reason was forged into dogma.

Darwin, in contrast, did not retain possession of his work. Battles were fought over the issues he raised, but his defenders were volunteers. No one was enlisted, and no one was compelled to follow a party line. There were no membership cards, no International Evolutionary Association. No one was prevented from furthering Darwin's work because of altering his theory. The discovery was attacked by institutions, but did not become institutionalized in defense. It was besieged by vested interests, but did not itself become a vested interest. Yet it survived, and has since participated widely in the ongoing process of science.

Without institutional protection the early discoveries of psychoanalysis might have been diluted or dispersed, never acquiring the usefulness they potentially held. But for such security the price was high. For when the issue is an idea, the institution that protects the infant is likely to stunt the child.

Even if institutional protection were needed in its infancy, certainly it is not needed now. Yet protection is still demanded. Institutions have their own "instinct" of survival, and do not fade away when their usefulness is at an end. As an institution psychoanalysis flourishes, and it presents its demands as the needs of science. It is said, for example, that the dividing line between psychoanalysis and psychotherapy must be kept clear; otherwise psychoanalysis may gradually merge with dynamic psychiatry and become indistinguishable from it. It is assumed to be self-evident that this would be bad. But why bad? And why is it a danger? If the dividing line is technological, then no institutional guarantees are needed for it to remain clear. Surgeons do not fear that surgery will blend with and become indistinguishable from first aid. If a surgeon applies a tourniquet, that's first aid; if a nurse performs an appendectomy, that's surgery. The nature of the procedure is a matter of fact and has nothing to do with the status of the performer. But if the dividing line between psychoanalysis and psychotherapy is ceremonial, then it is not scientific interests that are served by keeping it clear, but institutional interests. If a wafer and wine are administered by a priest, it's a sacrament; if by a layman, a sacrilege. The distinction depends on the status and appointments of the performer, having nothing to do with the nature of the performance. The distinction between psychoanalysis and dynamic psychiatry is coming to be of this kind. If psychoanalysis is performed by one who has not the status of an analyst, it is not recognized as analysis. Conversely, much of the work of analysts that falls far short of the minimum standards of analysis is freely designated and readily accepted as psychoanalysis.

The privacy of psychoanalysis is another factor that forces

it toward dogma. The therapeutic transaction is not open for inspection. The analyst and analysand can report what happens, but as both are involved neither can be disinterested. Except for rare tape-recorded sessions, the most direct view that any third person gains of the analytic process occurs during the course of training: the student analyst reports to the training analyst what happens, hour by hour. But even here the margin for distortion is wide. Not everything can be reported, and what is left out may be more important than what is transmitted.

Since the phenomena under consideration are not accessible to disinterested observers, the postulated relationships are not verifiable. This fosters conjectural excesses, and plausibility becomes the standard whereby conjecture acquires the status of truth. Such truth is precarious, and the effort to make it firm transforms it into dogma. Few Freudian analysts will, for example, publicly question the universality of the oedipus complex; for this "truth" has become dogma. Doubt acquires, thereby, the ring of heresy.

Science does not flourish under such conditions. From secrecy comes art or fraud, but not science. Burglary was diminished by street-lighting, embezzlement by double-entry bookkeeping, and dogma by the verifiability of reported truth. The privacy of psychoanalysis imposes such difficulties that many analysts despair of its ever being a science and consider it irrevocably an art. This disposes of the scientific pretentiousness and humbug, but clears the way for other abuses. For therapy by hunch is no more reliable than therapy by pseudo science. To abandon the search for verification is to abandon the search for truth.

The inaccessibility of the phenomena under investigation leads to an increasing interest in the character of the investigator. Analytic work cannot be judged on its merits, for it is not open to view. And precisely because it has always been inaccessible there are no generally accepted criteria by which to judge it. "In this business," it is said, "it's not what you know that counts, but what you are." A learned analyst may be a poor therapist, while one who has studied little may have a sure touch. What the analyst knows from books can be ascertained; but his application of that knowledge is in private and is largely unknown. For this reason attention comes to be focused on his character. Training analyses become more exhaustive, attempting to safeguard the quality of future performance by dealing more thoroughly with the character of the performer.

When scientific work comes to be judged by the character of the scientist, the work is not likely to remain scientific. For there is no reliable correlation between the character of the performer and the quality of his performance; and, even if there were, the standards whereby to measure what a man is are themselves arbitrary. This interest in the character of the analyst leads to a preoccupation with caste and status that is inimical to the development of psychoanalysis as a science.

The strongest influence toward dogma, however, is the demand for magic. Psychoanalysis has only insight to offer, but few persons come to it with the intention of using insight instrumentally. Knowledge of personality has increased enormously during the past fifty years, and much of this knowledge has become common information. This has not, however, created a greater feeling of competence in the handling of emotional problems. There is rather a greater reluctance to consider unhappiness as the manifestation of a problem to be handled on one's own, and a growing tendency to consider it the expression of an illness that warrants the intervention of an expert and the assumption of responsibility by him. There has occurred an enormous expansion of the concept of mental illness and a corresponding constriction in the concept of moral responsibility.[1]

In the analytic process the work of the analyst is, or tries to be, instrumental; the work of the patient purports to be instrumental, but is in fact largely institutional. This is the reason why so few analyzed persons are critical of psychoanalysis. Continued allegiance is the rule; virulent antagonism is not uncommon; but objective criticism is rare. Psychoanalysis does not claim infallibility; but it does claim to achieve, in carefully selected cases, radical character changes with dependable regularity. When it fails to do so, it is rare for the patient to face this fact simply and directly. If he blames psychoanalysis in general or his analyst in particular, his accusation is apt to be so partisan and bitter as to be worthless as evidence. More commonly, if he faces the fact of failure, he will blame himself and exonerate psychoanalysis. The most common outcome, however, is simply to pretend that the analysis was successful.

This is the phenomenon of the Emperor's Clothes; and

wherever it occurs it is an indication that the activity in question is institutional, in whole or in part. In the instrumental process no question is more pertinent than "Does it work?" In the institutional process this question is outlawed, and the answer is taken for granted: "Of course it works!" The failure of prayer to bring about what was prayed for does not revise the belief in the power of prayer. The evidence is simply ignored.

Events in the psychoanalytic process, however, are not so clear-cut; for analysis is an intricate intermingling of instrumental and institutional activities, and cannot be labeled simply one or the other. But, without any doubt, the Emperor of Psychoanalysis is sometimes naked—as all who are free to see, do see. Many persons—analysts as well as patients—are not free in this respect. By proclaiming itself clothed in the raiments of science psychoanalysis becomes acceptable to the sophisticated who search for magic. It seems to promise the transformation of self, to be the hidden door to all the lost certainties.

THE SOCIOLOGY OF TRANSFERENCE

Nothing is so characteristic of psychoanalysis as the feelings which the patient develops for the analyst. They are apt to be intense, and often they are strikingly at variance with the reality of the analyst's behavior, manner, appearance, and ability. They may be either positive or negative in quality. Analysts are generally more active in analyzing negative reactions than positive ones, however, and hence analysis is largely characterized by feelings of veneration and gratitude.

"No one else could possibly understand me so well as you";
"You sense the meaning of what I say almost before the words
have crossed my lips"—such expressions are commonplace. All
analysts know that various of their colleagues are blundering
and incompetent, and do not hesitate, in private, to say so; but
patients, who are in a uniquely favorable position to judge,
usually fail to see the obvious. Indeed, if analysts were rated
according to depositions taken from patients currently in a
state of positive feeling, one would find the profession to be
miraculously free of mediocrities. Each and every analyst
would prove to be a superb craftsman, the very best in the
field, and each and every patient would be uniquely fortunate
in having chanced to become a patient of that one analyst best
able to understand him. By his friends and his wife an analyst
is seen to have a full measure of shortcomings; but by his
patients he is perceived as a masterpiece of wisdom, tact, wit,
and kindness. When analyst and analysand are of different
sex, these feelings are usually augmented by elements of sexual
and romantic yearning. The propensity to idealize the analyst
is not a function of ordinary gullibility; for the clever and the
sophisticated are as vulnerable as the naïve.

Analysts take little comfort from this state of affairs, however; for adoration is the mask of dependence. Freud found it
a nuisance that his women patients fell in love with him; it
interfered with the work of understanding their neuroses.
Subjecting the interference itself to analysis, he discovered
that the professed feelings duplicated prior feelings toward
parents, that they did not originate in reference to him, but
had simply been transferred. The investigation of such trans-

ference feelings has since become the central aspect of psycho-analytic technique, and the resolution of transference a criterion for the completion of analysis.

If the patient's feelings toward his analyst duplicate his childhood feelings toward his parents, then clearly the super-ego must be involved as an intermediate step. For since the superego is the internalized representative of parents, the first transfer of feelings must have been from parents to superego. In this sense, the relationship of ego to superego is one of chronic internalized transference. The immediate source of the transference feelings of psychoanalysis is the feelings previously directed toward the superego. This does not, of course, imply that transference feelings abolish the superego—no more than it would imply that the establishment of the superego abolishes the child-parent relationship. It asserts only that the superego and the analyst are successive legatees to the original feelings and attitudes directed toward parents.

If this reasoning is correct, the change in the superego during the past fifty years must be reflected by a change in the social potential for transference feelings in analysis. The issue here is not the unique aspects of any one superego, but rather the social superego—a concept analogous to that of social character. This concept does not refer to a hypothetical superego of society as a whole. It continues to make reference to individuals, but only to those superego elements which are shared by a significantly large group. When one views the superego of an individual, one sees it as the incorporated images of parents; for it reflects the unique ways in which those particular parents gave praise and administered punishment. The faces disappear when one views the social superego; for there one sees only the shared elements—the ideals and faiths which that particular society holds dear, and hence wishes to preserve and perpetuate.

If, as has been maintained, the superego today is of diminished authority as compared to fifty years ago, it would follow that we are more vulnerable than our grandparents to the development of transference in psychoanalysis. For a superego of great authority makes a binding claim on the allegiance of the ego. Such a superego resists—and, if sufficiently strong, prevents—the transfer of this allegiance to another ideal, another cause, or another model.

History does not provide an experiment with which to test this inference directly; for psychoanalysis did not exist in the nineteenth century. An indirect test is possible, however, by virtue of the fact that there exist today persons who, so far as character and identity are concerned, are more representative of the last century than of the present one. These are persons whose values have survived intact the welter of contemporary change. They know who they are and where they're going and why, and what is worth struggling for and how much. A devout Catholic and a dedicated Marxist might serve as examples. It is unusual for such persons to consult a psychoanalyst, and when they do they are not liable to the development of that intense preoccupying yearning to which people of today are so vulnerable.

Appearances in such matters, however, may easily deceive. What appears to be strength and autonomy of superego may in fact be the superego's last-ditch effort to preserve itself against change. A superego is never more authoritarian than when its authority is about to be lost; conscience delivers its direst threats just before the commission of sin; and never do believers pray more fervently than when on the verge of abandoning belief in the efficacy of prayer. When superego strength is anchored in Catholic or Marxist ideology, and when this ideology has been undermined, the superego may appear to be strong while in fact being fragile. In such circumstances relatively slight contact with an analyst may precipitate the collapse of eternal verities and the consequent focusing upon the analyst of the displaced longings and aspirations.

The jealousy of the Church in regard to psychoanalysis is well founded. Analysts are inclined to minimize or deny the conflict, for practically never do they undertake to destroy the ideologies of their patients. They know that insight—which is all they have to offer—will be regarded as a sorry substitute for absolute value. Few persons can live by bread alone, and analysis offers nothing more than the bread of matter-of-fact problem-solving. Yet there is in fact a basic conflict. For analysis is the application of instrumental activity to the longing for parental protection and the quest for certainty which previously have been the province of institutional absolutes. In taking as its goal the resolution of transference, analysis strikes a blow at all irrational allegiances.

Rarely does a person whose superego strength is anchored in a genuinely firm ideology consult a psychoanalyst; and when he does, he is not so vulnerable to the development of transference feelings. Such persons are becoming rare these days; they were more characteristic of the last century than of this one. It may be inferred, therefore, that psychoanalysis could not have flourished in the nineteenth century, that the temper of America in the 1870's, of Victorian England, of Bismarck's Germany was incompatible with psychoanalysis, and that this incompatibility was a function of the social character that then prevailed. It is the loss of stable values and the inevitability of change that have made possible the luxuriant blossoming of psychoanalysis in the twentieth century. Neurotic suffering may have been as common in the last century as in this one, but the social character within which it occurred would not have lent itself to psychoanalytic ministrations. In this sense the growth of psychoanalysis must be understood, not simply in terms of its own progressive development as a science, but as a product of a particular culture that fosters that development. It is a symptom of our times.

Superego strength cannot be objectively measured, and hence is a relative concept. Thus far in this discussion it has been considered in relation only to the superego strength of preceding generations. It is relevant here, however, to consider it as relative to ego strength; for the strength of the superego is reciprocal to the strength of the ego. The relationship is not precisely reciprocal, as will become evident, but loosely so.

In individual patients the superego may exert greater authority than the ego will acknowledge or submit to, but this is the exception of neurosis rather than the rule of society. The social superego cannot exert greater authority than the social ego acknowledges. On the one hand is the stability of the ideals and values embedded in the superego; on the other hand is the ego's need for protection by the superego. These two are related. It is the ego's sense of weakness and peril, its need for security, and its quest for certainty that constitute the license and the warrant for superego authority. The superego can exist only as a function of these needs.

It is possible, however, for superego values to be lost in excess of the ego's ability to do without them. No one truly believes in God who does not need God; but many persons lose God before they are really able to live in an unprotected universe. The latter is the situation of our time: eternal verities have been lost in excess of our ability to get along comfortably without them. This leaves man's quest for certainty dangling loose, and creates the enormous current potential for transference.

It is now possible to relate the heightened current potential for transference to the process of cultural change. The accelerating instrumental process impacts more and more forcibly upon institutional absolutes. Ours has become a culture of change rather than a culture of tradition. As institutions give ground, the ideals upon which they have focused the aspirations of men are weakened. Some of these aspirations, which formerly were claimed by institutional absolutes, are now unattached. They form a reservoir of restless yearning and discontent. This is the source of mass movements, of the frightened retreat from reason, and of the transference manifestations of psychoanalysis.

Since transference feelings are irrational and since the potential for such feelings is currently increased, it might seem to follow that this is an age of unreason, that we are less rational than were our grandparents. No such conclusion is justified, however, by the foregoing considerations. The high current potential for transference feelings in analysis is new, but there is nothing new about irrational feelings. Transference is an irrational allegiance, but the allegiances which it succeeds and replaces were equally irrational and, moreover, were not so open to critical examination. Doctor Thurston would never have submitted to psychoanalysis; he would, indeed, have scorned the weakness of anyone who developed a prolonged dependent attachment to a physician. But, as has been mentioned, the relationship of the ego to a strong superego is, in itself, a kind of transference. It is internal and is compatible with a high degree of self-sufficiency, but is equally irrational. Doctor Thurston was involved in a more prolonged dependent relationship than are most analysands; for he was in bondage to the eternal verities imbedded in his superego— to God, to free private enterprise, to the Democratic Party, and the like. He who gives allegiance to such institutional values, without critical examination, simply because they have been valued in the past, is hardly qualified to pass judgment on the transference feelings of analysands.

The high potential for transference feelings, therefore, is no indication that we are becoming more irrational. Indeed, if the concept of transference be expanded to include internal transference—the dependent relationship of the ego to the superego's legacy from the past—it would appear that the diminished authority of the superego reflects an over-all reduction in the potential for transference. The continuing gains of the instrumental process constitute continuing gains of reliable information. The retreat from reason threatens this process—and in many areas of human endeavor has slowed it—but thus far has not brought it to a halt.

TRANSFERENCE TERMINABLE AND INTERMINABLE

The proposition that transference is a function of the loss of institutional absolutes does not conflict with the psychoanalytic view that transference is the irrational repetition of attitudes, feelings, and fantasies from the past. The phenomenon which in psychoanalysis is viewed as an individual development is here being viewed as a social development. The two propositions do not, in fact cannot, collide; for they exist on different levels of generalization. To assert the crystalline structure of table salt is not to deny that it is made up of molecules. The social theory of transference is related to the psychoanalytic theory in the same way that crystalline structure is related to molecular structure.[2] Some aspects of the phenomenon are explicable only by one theory, some only by the other; for transference is both an individual and a social phenomenon.

To inquire into the transference of an individual patient, to investigate why it assumes its own particular guise rather than some other, and why it changes on one certain day—to refer such queries to the temper of our times would be absurd. Such questions call for formulations of individual psychodynamics. Conversely, to investigate the changing patterns of neuroses, to probe the reasons for the currently heightened capacity for transference—to refer such issues to individual psychodynamics would be equally absurd. Such questions call for formulations of social change. It is phenomena of the latter order that are here being dealt with, and the theory being advanced asserts that the ideals and values of the last century largely absorbed the aspirations of men, and that, correspondingly, the present dearth of such ideals and values results in a reservoir of restless energy which is the source of the widening need for psychoanalysis and of the transference phenomenon which so prominently characterizes it.

Any phenomenon which has existence and structure at multiple levels calls for multiple theories. The danger lies not in the multiplicity of theories but in the mixing of levels of generalization. The chemist who asserts that a handful of salt is part molecular and part crystalline is guilty of an egregious lapse. The analyst who explains the transference of an individual patient partly in terms of individual psychodynamics and partly in terms of the environing culture blunders equally. The individual and the social do not divide between themselves one realm of discourse; each is a separate and complete realm of discourse. Transference, like any other aspect of human nature and conduct, is at the same time altogether individual and altogether social.

In psychoanalysis the individual level of generalization is always the relevant one. A culturally established trait and an individually produced symptom may be one and the same; but in undertaking psychoanalysis it is understood that the problem will be regarded as an individually produced symptom, that the solution will be sought in the alteration of the patient, not of society. This is true regardless of the degree to which the patient may have been victimized by social forces. Logically correct causal formulations for any symptom may be made in social terms, but—since the individual cannot materially alter his culture—such formulations are irrelevant. In attempting to reduce the incidence of crime in a community, the relevant causal statements would deal with slums, poverty, political corruption, and the like. But in treating an individual criminal, the relevant causal statements must deal with his impulsivity, his hatred of his father, his intolerance of delay, his infatuation with an ambitious girl, and the like. In the analysis of an individual, therefore, the environing culture is rightly considered an invariable, a force not subject to manipulation, and hence causally irrelevant to the patient on the couch and to the analyst behind the couch.

Psychoanalysis is often accused of shifting responsibility from the patient to his parents. In fact, it is usually patients, not analysts, who blame parents. For, though it does not help toward the solution of the problem, it may diminish the patient's feeling of guilt at doing nothing about it himself. Psychoanalysis attempts to locate full responsibility in the patient. This is not a matter of principle or of justice, but of function. It simply is of no avail to blame parents. Nothing happens. Parents cannot undo their ancient mistakes, and society will not adapt itself to an individual. If the patient cannot change himself, the problem will persist; and he cannot even begin to change himself according to plan until he assumes responsibility for his troubles. Psychoanalysis delves into childhood only in order that the patient may understand how his neurotic patterns originated, and may thereby perceive that his reactions are not consonant with current reality but are the senseless repetition of ancient modes. This understanding facilitates the substitution of choice for the state of being blindly driven.

In analytic work, therefore, the individual level of generalization is always the relevant one. The conflicts are re-experienced in the transference, and the analyst interprets this in terms of the patient's individual development. Sometimes this achieves the resolution of transference, and sometimes it does not. More commonly these days it does not.

When the analyst, alone in his study, takes up the question of why transference so often cannot be resolved—not with a specific patient, but with patients generally—he is dealing with a problem of a different kind, one toward the solution of which a consideration of individual psychodynamics cannot contribute. This is a problem on the social level of generalization. It involves the relationship of psychoanalysis to the kinds of emotional problems to which people of today are vulnerable. It is to this problem that the social theory of transference is addressed.

In a stable society the magical hopes of men are bound to institutional absolutes, and the social potential for transference feelings in analysis is low. Such a potentiality may be individually created, however, by the onset of neurosis. When an individual of such a society suffers a disabling neurotic conflict and undertakes psychoanalysis, he begins to feel toward his analyst as he formerly felt toward some significant person of the past, usually a parent. In reference to the neurotic conflict the analyst is, or tries to be, neutral; he attempts to remain emotionally equidistant from the conflicting forces. In the experience of the patient, however, he is partisan. In the patient's attempt to regain a lost sense of security, the analyst is drawn into the conflict. If he is perceived as a destroyer, the patient tries to defeat him; if he is perceived as a savior, the patient tries to win his love. This is the classical form of transference, and it yields to analysis. The steps are familiar: the analyst demonstrates that the feelings directed toward him cannot be accounted for in terms of his real behavior and characteristics; the original object of these feelings is revealed through dreams and associations; the crucial experiences with that person are recalled; and the conflict is worked through. The energy that was bound up in the conflict is freed for reinvestment in goal-directed activity.

No one is altogether free of unconscious conflict, and to the extent that it is present and can be analyzed, transference can be resolved or diminished. In these days, however, more and more often the aspirations directed toward the analyst are the product, not of unconscious conflict, but of the loss of the eternal verities which formerly bound these aspirations. This culturally determined loss of institutional absolutes creates the same potential for transference as exists when security is lost by unconscious conflict. There is the same propensity to direct toward the analyst the yearning, the fear, and the hate. In these circumstances transference cannot be analytically resolved. For psychoanalysis does not surmount culture, but is part of it. It provides no escape from culturally determined problems.

The old ideals are undermined, the aspirations are unattached, and identity is impaired or lost. With increasing frequency this predicament leads to psychoanalysis. It seems to offer a solution, to be the key that will free and enrich the imprisoned and impoverished inner man, that will unleash creative effort and provide meaning to life. Many persons reckon it their best as well as last hope, the most radical attack on the problem. "If this doesn't work, nothing will work."

It does work when the problem of identity is secondary to neurosis. Values may be dispersed and identity obscured by unconscious conflict. When such is the case, psychoanalysis may find the lost pattern and bring together the scattered elements. It then appears to have created the identity, to have provided the meaning and the purpose to life, whereas it has in fact only removed an encumbrance. Such conditions were more common in the last century, when society so actively supported a pattern of values that an analyst might safely assume an apparent lack of identity to be secondary to neurosis. Many analysts retain this orientation, approaching present-day patients with a nineteenth-century conception of social character, assuming that values persist unchanged and that the only significant variable is individual psychodynamics.

Nowadays the lack of identity is more often secondary only to the collapse of institutional absolutes—of goals, values, and ideals. So far as individual psychodynamics is concerned, it is a primary disorder. In this condition—adrift and without compass, lacking even a sense of destination—more and more people seek through psychoanalysis an answer to the question, "Who am I?" It is known to expose deeper feelings, to unmask pretenses, and hence it becomes plausible to assume that it will uncover, also, one's true self. This asks too much of a procedure which is, even by name, analytic. It could uncover an identity provided such were hidden, but cannot create one that is lacking. It could expose a pattern of values, a philosophy of life, provided such were repressed; but these things are not likely to be found in the unconscious. It is usually the other way round: a sense of identity, a pattern of values, a philosophy of life—these are the agents for the repression of other elements of mental life. They are—except in mass movements —built slowly in the course of one's life and, once formed, are rarely repressed. Impulses, fears, defenses, anxiety—these are the things that get repressed, and these are the things that are exposed in therapy.

For psychoanalytic treatment is a technique of investigation, not a way of life. To undertake psychoanalysis in quest for identity is to pursue an illusion. What one achieves is not identity, but a more sensitive awareness of thoughts and feelings. Since psychoanalysis provides no goals, this extended awareness is likely to be used for the furtherance of the same old mode, namely adjustment. What gets reinforced is precisely that from which one wished to escape, the domination of life by the process of keeping in step. Analyzed persons may keep in step with groups characterized by sophisticated disdain of conventional curbs on impulse and idea, but this should not deceive; conformity is conformity, whether it be to Southern Methodism or to existentialism.

VI ⎰ VALUE

THE PROBLEM OF VALUE

Values determine goals, and goals define identity. The problem of identity, therefore, is secondary to some basic trouble about value. The existence of such trouble is generally recognized, and it is considered an urgent problem of our time. Scientists, however, have been inclined to sidestep it. Wishing to keep the field of empirical work uncluttered, they have usually relegated such problems to moralists and philosophers. This position is becoming untenable. If the scientist restricts his interest and responsibility to the laboratory, it will fall to the lot of others to determine the value of his findings and the ends they are to serve. And, in fact, the "others" will not usually be moralists or philosophers, but men of action. The scientist is becoming less willing, in particular, to leave such decisions to politicians or to the blind uses of tradition and institution. In this respect psychology is in the same position as the other sciences. If the issue of identity is of crucial importance for our

time, and if, as has been maintained, the problem of identity is
secondary to the problem of value, then psychology must deal
with value.

"Collapse of values" has become a cliche, used without documentation and without challenge. In some way everyone senses
what is meant, but the issue is vague. Values are legion, and not
all of them are collapsing. The field of value is coextensive
with the field of human endeavor, and it is by no means obvious
that organized human activity is coming to an end. Tools have
value for a mechanic, and food and shelter and friendship have
value for everyone. About these things there is no confusion.
Values, clearly, cannot be simply lumped together; for they
exist on different levels. One can say very little about food
and shelter that applies equally well to Christianity and democracy. Values are structured in a hierarchy. Different or-
ders of value, therefore, require different treatment.

Divorce presents a frequent and typical value problem of
our time. Upon considering divorce for the purpose of marry-
ing someone else, one must choose between conflicting values.
On the one hand are loyalty, faithfulness, attachment to children, and the like; on the other, love, intimacy, and the mutual
enrichment of life which the new relationship seems to promise. There is no uncertainty about the merit of either group;
both are prized and held dear. It is for precisely this reason that
the rising divorce rate is subject to such divergent interpretations. It may be taken as evidence that primary ties are being
held capriciously, that presumably binding commitments are
being made tentatively, and hence that a moral deterioration is

under way. It may also be seen as evidence of a mounting reluctance to endure an impoverished life and a barren relationship, and a new freedom to seek a fuller life and a richer relationship. The value problem is real, but it is not a problem of determining which set of values is real and which illusory. Both are real. The problem is one of how to choose between values which are, in the existing circumstances, incompatible.

One may attempt an arithmetical summation, but it is hard to weigh loyalty against love. Deep-lying motivations are involved, not all of which are accessible; the quantities assigned to these motivations are arbitrary and may change with one's mood. The calculus of love and loyalty is faulty, and the decision feels unstable. In such a situation one wishes, rather, to turn to a value that is superordinate to those in conflict. The Catholic religion is such a value, and is well designed to adjudicate the issue. For those who have no such higher value to which to refer the case, the decision is more difficult. However it is decided, it may engender haunting misgivings.

The example of divorce locates the problem in the field of value: the trouble is at the top. Religions, ideologies, philosophies, and all comprehensive codes, patterns, and world views —these are the values that have been undermined. They are the highest in the sense of having been designed to rule over all other values and to resolve all value conflicts. The confusion, uncertainty, and, occasionally, collapse of values at this level, therefore, is reflected in troubled value judgments at all lower levels.

Values at the top of the hierarchy are, in effect, patterns of value, since they comprehend and organize subordinate values.

They may be explicit as, for example, Christianity and Communism are explicit and codified; or they may be implicit and unformulated, as is the case whenever unified and integrated mores insure a traditional way of life. Both types of comprehensive value patterns have in our time been undermined.

The crucial question of value is judgmental: What things *should* men prize and hold dear? The discussion which follows is preliminary to this question, and in it the point of view is empirical. Those things which men *do* prize and hold dear are termed values—without reference to their validity. Where effort and devotion and allegiance are committed, there value resides for those who so commit their energies.

THE NATURE OF VALUE

Values are products of the life process and are coextensive with this process. They do not exist in a void, but are engendered by the activities of men. No values transcend man in origin, though many transcend the evidence at hand. The belief in God goes beyond scientific knowledge, but it does not go beyond man. It is a product of man's religious, ceremonial, and myth-making activities. Transcendental values, therefore, like all other values, arise from and are perpetuated by the activities of men.

Value is a product of sustained and purposeful activity, rather than casual and random activity. The following example is both commonplace and representative. A man cares nothing about rugs, and upon leaving the house of a friend would be unable to say, if he were asked, whether the floor covering had been a straw mat or a priceless Kashan. Because his wife loves Persian rugs, however, he decides to get one for her as a birthday present. Upon making inquiry, he is surprised at the prices and, wishing to get the best for his money, goes from dealer to dealer, examining, listening, comparing, touching. Thereafter rugs have some importance for him. Upon entering a strange house he is apt to notice the rugs, and is apt, moreover, to know the difference between a Bokhara and a Shiraz and to appreciate their unique qualities. His activity has generated value.

Value is a product, not only of activity, but also of choice. We do not value all things that we deal with and produce. Certain things or conditions or experiences are seen as "better than" certain others. This perception and decision are essential to the emergence of value.

As the activities of man may be characterized as tool-using and as myth-making, the values which derive from them may be likewise characterized. The values which derive from tool-using retain the characteristics of the instrumental process, and the values which derive from myth-making retain the characteristics of the institutional process. A wheelbarrow is better than a handbarrow for transporting heavy loads; a rifle is better than bow and arrow for killing buffalo; for conveying the quality of human life and the range and subtlety of human relationships the novels of Tolstoy are better than the novels of A. J. Cronin—these are instrumental valuations; and the values which thereby accrue to wheelbarrows, to rifles, and to Tolstoy are instrumental values. "Better than," in the instrumental process, refers to relative adequacy of function for an implied or specified purpose.

Christianity is better than Buddhism; the monogamous family is better than any other possible arrangement for the regulation of sex and the rearing of children; the private practice of medicine is, whatever the circumstances, better than socialized medicine—these are institutional valuations, and the values which thereby accrue to Christianity, to the monogamous family, and to private practice are institutional values. "Better than," in the institutional process, means "more in accord with the dominant institutional directives."

Institutional values derive from the activities associated with myth, mores, and status. The choice involved purports to be final. Such values do not refer to, but transcend, the evidence at hand. They claim absolute status and immunity to change, but are, in fact, relative to the culture that supports them: Christian sacraments are without validity in India, and suttee has achieved no validity in the western world. The final authority of such values is force.

Instrumental values derive from tool-using, observation, and experimentation, and hence are temporal, matter-of-fact, and secular. They do not transcend the evidence at hand, but derive from progressively refined attention to such evidence. They possess transcultural validity: for red man as well as white man, a rifle is better than a bow and arrow. They are, however, relative to the state of empirical knowledge at any given time, and change as that knowledge is enlarged. The final authority of such values is reason.

At any time, in any individual or any society, values are of these two kinds; for no one is altogether free of institutional values, and no one is devoid of instrumental values. The proportion, however, is subject to change. Many values fall into both categories and may be defended by both camps. The trait of honesty, for example, is an instrumental value insofar as its authority derives from the observation that it dependably fosters desired consequences; it is an institutional value insofar as it is beyond revision and its authority independent of observed consequences.

CLAIMS AND COUNTERCLAIMS

Value discussions are characterized by invidious claims and counterclaims. These involve such issues as ends and means, intrinsic and extrinsic, higher and lower. Underlying all of these polarities is the continuing tension between the instrumental process and the institutional process.

For those who stand closer to the institutional process, who locate their security in its guarantees, the distinction between ends and means is of fundamental importance. Science and technology have value, it is said, but merely as means. Indeed, as Dewey has pointed out, the adjective "mere" is, in such discussions, a ubiquitous modifier of instrumental values. Real or true value resides in ends, and the ends in question are not mediate but final. They are fantasied oceans toward which the river of mankind is, or should be, flowing. They are variously described as the ideal, the spiritual, or the historically inevitable. They partake of the absolute, and they bear such titles as Heaven, Salvation, Communism, or The Ultimate Perfectibility of Man. They are conceived to be the termini of man's journey through life, both as an individual and as a species. Without such a final destination in mind, progress is declared impossible and the journey meaningless. The values of all things are determined by their estimated bearing on movement toward this ultimate end.

For those who locate their security and identity more largely in the instrumental process, the duality of ends and means diminishes to a distinction, depending upon nothing more than whether activities are being viewed at short range or long range. What is means to an end must itself become an end if it is to be taken seriously; and the long range end will itself become, eventually, a means to something beyond. The progress of man is seen as a progression. Not only is it independent of final ends, it is in fact incompatible with such ends. As the series 2-4-8-16-32 . . . is, by its nature, open ended, so the progress of man is deemed inconsistent with any final state. Admittedly a stellar accident or a man-made catastrophe might terminate life on this planet; but such a terminus is not inherent in the instrumental process. A stellar accident would be beyond man's control; a world-wide atomic war would be attributed, not to man's discovery of atomic energy, but to the misuse of this discovery by institutions. This point of view is associated with Dewey, who has demonstrated most cogently that the ends we achieve are very much like the means we employ.

For the institutionalist, another distinction of similar importance and similar implications is that between intrinsic and extrinsic value. A state of joy or of sexual pleasure, for example, is considered to possess innate value, independent of the context in which it occurs. The instrumentalist would, again, diminish the distinction. The value to be ascribed to such states depends, he would maintain, upon their antecedents and consequences, upon their place in and continuity with the life process. The state of joy which derives from the use of heroin is evaluated differently from that which follows the solution of a difficult problem. The state of sexual pleasure which occurs in a casual orgy is evaluated differently from that which occurs in an ongoing relationship. Value is not independent of instinctual needs, but the gratification of such needs does not establish a category of intrinsic value.

Institutional values are generally regarded as higher, more important, than instrumental values. The distinction is invidious if it is taken to mean that institutional values are, by their nature, higher. Nothing of this sort is here implied, and the distinction is empirical: any value which organizes, directs, and integrates other values is, in respect to those other values, higher. The question is the nature of those values which are highest in this sense, and without doubt they are mostly institutional. The arguments which become really heated, the disputes which break friendships, the issues which lead to war, the beliefs for which one is willing to die—these usually concern institutional values. The person who said that fundamental differences in values can be settled, if at all, only by a bashing in of heads [1] was, beyond any doubt, referring to institutional values.

Clashes between instrumental values seldom invoke violence. Wheelbarrows are alleged to be better than handbarrows, but never has a debate over this issue led to bloodshed. Wheelbarrow users are not apt to care much if handbarrow users stick to their old ways. And handbarrow users are apt to be curious about the new contrivance and want to see how it works and to try it. If it works better, they will use it. In such differences the appeal is rational, and one turns to the evidence.

If handbarrows should be institutionalized—as would be likely if they were used, for example, primarily for the ritual transportation of the dead—the introduction of wheelbarrows might then lead to violence. This would not, however, be a clash of instrumental values, but a clash of instrumental value with institutional value. The products of the instrumental process are, indeed, constantly being institutionalized. When a technological advance seriously breaches an institution, the institution destroys the invader if it can. If it cannot, it may heal itself by incorporating the weapon which made the wound. The Ptolemaic conception of the universe, originally a product of the instrumental process, was institutionalized by the Christian church and, when challenged by the theory of Copernicus and the evidence of Galileo, was defended by the Inquisition, not as scientific theory, but as dogma. A relative instrumental value had been converted into an absolute institutional value.

Of more significance, however, is the fact that for the most important decisions of life the instrumental process provides no clear-cut answers. Usually it provides the basis for a partial answer, but one so tentative, so hedged with conditions, so threatened by the possible effect of unreckoned or unmeasured variables that one is prone to discard the incomplete segment of instrumental value and to make one's decision on the basis of an institutional value of comprehensive scope which claims certainty. It's good to know that wheelbarrows are better than handbarrows, but this knowledge seems trivial when the issue is one of sin and salvation. In comparison, instrumental values appear to merit the adjective "mere," seem indeed to belong to an inferior realm. In the crucial problems of life the data are complex and equivocal. The evidence is variously interpreted, even by those who approach it from an instrumental point of view. A dozen psychoanalysts listening to the same case material are likely to formulate a dozen different estimations of its unconscious meaning, of its prognostic significance, and of the specific interpretation which should be made. Yet they may share the same hypotheses and the same empirical approach. There is some common ground, some area of "consensual validation," but it is far less extensive than psychoanalytic literature would suggest. Similar instrumental uncertainty exists in all such borderline areas—in marriage and child rearing, government and economics, war and peace. It is at just such junctures, where the known is interlaced with the unknown, that scientific progress takes place and the area of the known is extended. It is extended but slowly in those fields where institutional pressure opposes each scientific advance; it is extended with accelerating velocity in those areas which are free of such opposing pressure. But the awareness of progress provides no present answer, and some problems will not wait. One must choose and act. In such circumstances, decisions are apt to be made by reference to institutional values. One prays, consults dogma, or refers—perhaps unwittingly—to mores. In psychological terms, the ego abandons the conflict and appeals to the superego for a verdict.

THE RECIPROCAL RELATIONSHIP

Science must frequently admit ignorance, but the institutional process is never at a loss. Those persons who live by institutions are guaranteed a complete set of values—from adultery to international relations, from gambling to child-rearing. Institutional values reign in all those areas of human endeavor, decision, and choice in which problem-solving, matter-of-fact, empirical methods have not as yet provided valid answers. In principle there has never been, as it were, any unclaimed territory in the realm of value. Where the surveyors of science are unable to penetrate, the institutional map-makers experience no difficulty. Throughout the entire course of human history they have always been able to come up with a detailed chart of any unexplored area of human choice. Instrumental and institutional values bear, therefore, a reciprocal relationship to each other. The one can expand only at the expense of the other.

The long-range trend of this relationship is unmistakable: institutional values give way and are replaced by instrumental values. The process is marked by vicissitudes, for institutional values are vigorously defended. Often, indeed, they attack and sometimes carry the day—as Galileo was forced to recant—but sooner or later they give way. Many of us, at one time, believed that God created man out of clay in the course of an ordinary day about 4000 B. C.; now we believe that there was no sudden act of creation, but that man has evolved from simpler forms of life in a continuous process extending over millions of years. The first belief did not, and does not, have general validity, but is relative to the institutions of Christendom, having cogency only where those institutions prevail. The second belief is based on scientific investigation, is relative to nothing but the state of scientific knowledge, and has transcultural validity. The replacement of the first belief by the second exemplifies the trend. The lives of most adults now living encompass many such shifts. Since the instrumental process proceeds at an accelerating rate, the replacement of institutional values by instrumental values is likewise an accelerating progression.

Instrumental values do not, however, replace institutional values in a one-to-one ratio. The evolutionary account replaces the Christian myth; but at the same time it undermines, without replacing, many of the sanctions, promises, and consolations of religion, all of which have value. In this manner the instrumental process destroys institutional values inadvertently, providing little or nothing in exchange. The family, with its cluster of associated values, has been weakened during the past fifty years. This has come about, not because science has challenged the family with a new and more efficient social grouping, but because of indirect and unplanned effects of the instrumental process. The revolution in communications has diminished the authority of parents, and the revolution in transport has weakened primary ties. But neither of these effects was intended, and nothing is offered in specific replacement of what was lost.

In our time, therefore, there *is* unclaimed territory in the field of value. *De jure*, there is none; in principle, institutional values are unchanged, and apologists for family, church, and state admit no loss of ground. But values cannot function as values unless they are held as such. A value which is forgotten or ignored is, empirically, not a value. Libraries are filled with eternal verities which can no longer be found in the hearts of living men.

The existence of such unclaimed territory does not, however, imply that institutions now melt away before technological advance, that they retreat before being challenged. They do now what they have always done; they stand their ground and fight, and yield only under duress. Institutional values derive from the institutional process, but are not identical with myth, mores, and institutions. Likewise, instrumental values derive from the instrumental process, but are not identical with the discoveries of science, the achievements of art, or the advances of technology. Values, that is, stand once removed from the activities which engender them. Therefore, while the clash of technology with institutions is hand-to-hand fighting, the opposing lines of instrumental and institutional values are separated by a no-man's-land of widening extent. It is not a trackless waste, but the tracks are so numerous, so winding, so superimposed one upon another, that no man can find his way with any certainty.

Psychoanalysts, particularly, are keenly aware of this no-man's-land; for patients apply to them for values which analysis cannot provide. Patients assume the opposing lines of value to be in contact, that such ground as is lost by one side is gained by the other. If religion no longer has the answers, psychoanalysis is bound to have them. Where institutional consolations are lost, the new science of man must have concocted a more effective balm for discontent. For how else, one wonders, could the old certainties have been allowed to slip away? Whatever values one has lost which derived from religion, patriotism, family, mores, and a traditional way of life, these values, the patient assumes, are replaceable by new and better values devised by scientific psychology. These expectations cannot be met. They derive only in part from exaggerated claims made by psychoanalysis; in larger part they derive from the wishful thinking of those who suffer and are confused. It is another guise of the ancient quest for certainty.

THE SOCIAL BASIS OF VALUE

The meaning of the instrumental process is clear: it provides for man's wants and secures him against danger. But the meaning of the institutional process is obscure. Dewey considers it to be a response to the same circumstances which call forth the instrumental process. It is, he suggests, simply one of the two methods of "dealing with the serious perils of life." [2] Ayres doubts that the institutional process was ever meant to protect man from the hazards of nature, but regards it as having been designed and used, from the very beginning, for exploitation —to invoke fear and seize power, to create status, to exert coercion, and to exact tribute.[3]

While these views are divergent as to the primary meaning of the institutional process, both designate actual uses to which it is put. For much of magic and superstition explicitly claims to ward off danger; and, likewise, these same myths have been used to exploit. It is possible, however, that, while the institutional process is used in both of these ways, neither of these uses accounts for its existence nor states its essential relevance to the condition of man.

The institutional process is the response of man to alienation and to mortality. As man becomes aware of himself as apart from his environment and as separate from his fellow men, the original oneness of life with its matrix is lost. To be aware of the separateness of self is to be aware of one's insignificance and helplessness, and this entails the knowledge that one will die. A modern rifle fells any beast, penicillin destroys microscopic assailants, but death remains. Eventually nothing avails against it, for it is not a misfortune but an inevitability.

The manhood of man depends upon his alienation and his awareness of mortality. Without them he would be less than human; for they are the perils, not of nature, but of the human condition. Against them the instrumental process is powerless. Indeed, the progress of the arts and sciences has been accompanied by increasing alienation and an ever-clearer awareness of mortality. To these aspects of the human condition, unamenable to instrumental solution, the institutional process is addressed.

Animism replaces the indifferent and inanimate universe with one peopled with human spirits and activated by human intentions. Magic replaces the helplessness of man with the omnipotence of God. All institutions assert a collectivity superordinate to the individual, a larger unity of which the individual is a part, to which he owes allegiance, and from which he gains a sense of security. This is most particularly true of religions. "The idea of society," wrote Durkheim, "is the soul of religion." [4] In religion, alienation is denied by a theory which makes us all children of God. It is denied in practice by ritual and ceremony, collectively performed, which assert in action the inclusion of the individual in a larger unity. In these ways the separateness of self is replaced by the brotherhood of man. The plain fact of death is declared to be an illusion: what appears as death is but the transition to larger living. In such ways the institutional process, in all of its various forms, ministers to the alienation of man and to his fear of dying. In so doing, incidentally, it creates the conditions for exploitation and bondage; for men have generally been willing, and even eager, to enslave themselves to any institution which promises solace on these scores.

The idea of society is equally intrinsic to the instrumental process. The scientist working alone in his laboratory is dependent upon the scientific findings of his predecessors, upon the craftsmen who produce the equipment and materials he uses, upon the publishers who make known his findings, and upon his colleagues who test them. Except for the society of which it is a part, his work would have no meaning; it would not, in fact, be possible. The same is true of the watchmaker working at his craft and of the writer constructing a novel. Any individual instance of instrumental activity is possible only by virtue of the instrumentally functioning society of

which the individual effort is a part. Neither the instrumental
process nor the institutional process could exist upon the basis
of a collection of isolated individuals, however numerous. Both
equally presuppose the existence of an organic society.

There is a difference, however, in the way in which they
make reference to social unity. The instrumental process takes
it for granted; the institutional process makes it a gospel. Continuously and tirelessly institutions assert the existence of a
social reality superordinate to the individual, declare that this
social entity alone has meaning, and that an individual life acquires significance only by virtue of the individual's finding
his place and identity in this larger whole. Nor are institutions
content with assertions. The idea is given tangible existence in
repeated collective actions—ritual, ceremony, rite, and sacrament. It comes about, therefore, that the idea of the social
organism as the locus of meaning and authority seems to be
the unique creation of the institutional process.

The meaning of life—for most persons, in all ages—has been
expressed in social terms. One's individual life is seen to have
significance by virtue of its participation in a larger whole the
significance of which is guaranteed by the institutional process.
The "meaning of life" has had an infinite variety of referents,
but throughout the ages these referents have all fallen within
the institutional process. A meaningful life for a monarchist is
to be one of the king's men; for a Christian, to be one of God's
children; for a Marxist, to fight at the barricades.

As institutional values are undermined, therefore, the meaning of life appears to be lost. The alienated person finds little

significance in his isolated life. He may, indeed, doubt that it is worth while even to continue living. Institutional patterns proclaim themselves to be the very foundation of social unity, and as these patterns are destroyed the idea of society is lost. The individual may then no longer recognize the existence of society as an organism which has meaning and authority. He is thrown back on his own resources, becomes himself the referent of meaning and value.

But what meaning and value can then be found? A single life is framed by birth and death; and how can an individual, foregoing reference to anything beyond himself, integrate meaningfully the facts of his life with the fact of his inevitable death? It is the very nature of protoplasm to rebel against it. For the alienated man, death is the final defeat which casts an ironic shadow over whatever minor victories may precede it.

From a cosmic point of view—a hypothetical consciousness which takes all of space and time as its referent—the entire life of man on this planet is meaningless, being but as a season of locusts; the social point of view appears to have been invalidated by the fall of institutional absolutes; and from an individual point of view life is absurd. There is no meaning beyond mere existence, and even the abstention from suicide is difficult to justify. One may commit one's life to passion or violence or conquest, but this too is absurd; and even the dignity and courage with which one may face death is absurd. There is no escape from the absurd for the man who foregoes illusions and sees life clearly. This is the position at which the existentialists arrive and which is stated most movingly by Camus.[5]

With this position the argument of this book takes issue. For
though the idea of society is the soul of the institutional process, it is the very essence, also, of the instrumental process. The
fall of institutional patterns, therefore, does not preclude value
and meaning at the social level. It is only because histories
record primarily the vicissitudes of institutional conflict that
the life of man on earth is a chaotic story of foolishness and
destruction. Divested of all institutional patterns, the life of
man would portray the organic unity of the instrumental
process, the continuity of arts and of technology. This process
is one of increasing knowledge and control. It has no terminus,
but it has direction; and this direction is away from ignorance,
superstition, cruelty, and helplessness. Individual life has value
and meaning by virtue of its participation in this process. The
fact of death, in this view, is reconcilable with the activities of
life; for a social process of which the individual was a part, to
which he has contributed, and with which he can identify,
survives his individual extinction. Indeed, without individual
mortality the instrumental process could not exist. For if no
one died, then soon no one could be born; and growth and
development would pass from the experience of mankind. The
progress of man is thus contingent upon the succession of generations.

No one would deny that the instrumental process has continuity, but many persons would deny that it has meaning. It
has growth and pattern, they would say, like a tree; but like a
tree it has no inherent meaning. Meaning is imposed upon it

by the faiths and ideals of the institutional process. The argument of this point of view might continue along the following line.

In determining that wheelbarrows are better than handbarrows the question, "Better for whom?" hardly needs to be asked, for the answer is obvious. Wheelbarrows are better for everyone, white man and black man, European and Asiastic. In the most crucial questions of value, however, the referent is not so clear. Just whose interests are to be considered? Whose welfare is to be promoted? Often these questions are not asked. One adopts automatically a predetermined referent and assumes that others will do likewise. But there is, in fact, wide variation; and unacknowledged differences concerning the referent of value lead to intractable quarrels about value itself. If three people are attempting to determine the best of several possible political actions and if one person is concerned with what would be best for General Motors, another with what would be best for the United States, and the third with what would be best for mankind, it is unlikely that they will reach an agreement. It is unlikely, also, that their disagreement can be resolved simply by a more detailed examination of the various measures under consideration; for the source of their disagreement is in their unspoken assumptions. This type of conflict, it is claimed, does not lend itself to instrumental solution. It can be solved only by the application of an *a priori* principle, for example, the golden rule. Such a principle is not an explanation, but an imperative. It states a value but offers no justification. Its validity is by fiat, by faith, or by the authority of Christ.

Ethical principles promulgated and defended by the institutional process are not, however, necessarily alien to the instrumental process. They may have a validity which is demonstrable, which is subject to empirical verification and explanation, and which can sustain them after the institutional absolutes upon which they have formerly rested have fallen into disrepute. The golden rule need not necessarily be conceded to the institutional process; for, in some considerable measure, it is the logic of art and technology as well as of faith and salvation.

To love one's neighbor as one's self means to consider his welfare along with one's own, to feel so identified with him that joint interest rather than personal interest becomes the referent of value. But why, from an instrumental point of view, should one love his neighbor? And how far does the neighborhood extend? It includes, certainly, the person next door. Does it include also the Cossacks of the Don and the savages of New Guinea?

Clearly there are limits, for the referent of value is finite. It does not include the entire universe. Seldom, if ever, does it refer to a grouping larger than the whole of mankind. We believe in kindness to animals and form societies to that end, but do not extend to animals the rights we reserve for ourselves. When it comes to the tubercle bacillus we grant it no rights whatsoever, but would regard its generic extermination as a value—a value, that is, for mankind, not for the tubercle bacillus.

But if the neighborhood is finite, just how is one to determine its boundaries? Some persons we consider to be of narrow or selfish nature: their valuations refer only to themselves, their immediate families, or their social classes. Others of more generous disposition may include all of mankind in their judgments of the good. The question here is one of evaluating the basis upon which evaluations are made, of determining the value of the referent of value. Is it a matter of temperament or faith, or do these questions lend themselves to empirical answers? If reason does not reach an end here, just how does it proceed?

Value judgments must refer to the welfare of one's neighbor for the reason that one's neighbor and one's self comprise a social organism, and that which injures a part of this organism injures the whole. The limits of the neighborhood are the limits of the social organism; that is to say, the referent of value extends to the limit of the social organism which is involved, and no further. The first of these assertions is generally acknowledged and requires no documentation. The second calls for some clarification.

Obviously there is not just one social organism, but an immense complexity of social entities existing in both parallel and hierarchical relationship. Each value judgment refers to one or another of these groupings, and it is of some importance that the referent be the relevant one. Often this is so obvious that no deliberation is called for. In evaluating several possible trips for a family vacation, the referent of value is the family—its interests, its pleasures, its needs. No larger social entity need be considered, for none is likely to be affected. If the Taft-Hartley bill is being evaluated, the referent of value is the entire United States. (At this point ambiguities appear, and one's unthinking assumptions may be mistaken. A physician in California may fail to see that he is a part of a social organism which includes the automobile workers of Detroit; for the impersonality of the medium of exchange conceals an essential relatedness. Yet he is, in fact, engaged in a cooperative enterprise with these automobile workers. He exchanges medical services for automobiles, and if the workers of Detroit should stop making automobiles no amount of money would then buy one.) In the determination of American policy in the Near East, the logical referent of value would be the whole of mankind.

Five hundred years ago the peoples of Western Europe were unaware even of the existence of the civilizations of the Incas and the Aztecs. It was not possible, therefore, for them to take the peoples of the western hemisphere into account in their value judgments. Now they can leave them out of account only at their grave risk; for what happens in the Americas now has profound effects on the peoples of Western Europe and, indeed, the entire world. Likewise, there may at this time be intelligent creatures similar to ourselves existing on a neighboring planet. If so, we are not now much concerned, nor need we be; for an event which occurs to their advantage or detriment does not affect us. They are not, in short, a part of our social organism, and hence there is no need for us to take them into account. If, however, it should come about in time that we of this earth and they of their planet should cooperate in the regulation of interplanetary space, then to just that extent our interests would become their interests and theirs ours. The social organism of which we are a part would have expanded, and it would then behoove us to extend the basis of our value judgments to include their welfare.

Such developments, if they occur, are in the future. But of urgent importance in the present is the recognition of that institutional fallacy which would limit the referent of value to the boundaries of national states. Those persons who honor the sentiment "My country, right or wrong" are claiming that the limits of the social organism shall not be deemed to exceed the limits of national sovereignty. But it is clear beyond all doubt that the instrumental process has created an interrelatedness and interdependence among the peoples of the world that makes all of mankind a single social organism, despite the fact that political institutions have not yet yielded to this instrumental fact.

The idea of society is intrinsic to the instrumental process, and this process steadily increases the size of the social organism. It is to this fact that John Donne gives recognition in saying, "And therefore never send to know for whom the bell tolls; It tolls for thee." For if one is close enough to hear the bell, it is likely that one's self and the man for whom it is sounding are parts of the same social organism. At present we are instrumentally in a position to hear the tolling of the bell from the most remote corners of the earth.

VALUE AND IDENTITY

Everyone agrees that a wheelbarrow is better than a handbarrow, but not everyone would agree that a rifle is better than a bow and arrow. This is, as it were, a loaded example, and the smoke of emotion quickly obscures the issue. One line of rea-

soning proceeds as follows. As a rifle is better than bow and
arrow for killing buffalo, it is better, also, for killing men.
Indian raids are trouble enough if the palisades are pierced by
arrows, but the trouble increases considerably with the thud of
bullets. Likewise, war between states, which is a disaster with
rifles, becomes a catastrophe with atomic bombs. In what
sense, then, are rifles and atomic bombs "better than" the
weapons which they replace? Does it make sense to ascribe
value to that which will be used destructively? Hostile relations with another state may "force" us to manufacture atomic
bombs and possibly to use them; but, in view of the probable
consequences, perhaps the discovery of atomic energy itself
should be considered a colossal misfortune.

The question is where to place the blame, and at this point
it is usual to speak of the "problems created by technological
progress." Since the trouble is an outcome of the discrepancy
between technology and institutions, it could be designated,
with equal accuracy, as the "problems created by institutional
rigidities and coercions." But this formulation is rare. Technology does not easily take offense, but institutions are sensitive. We easily criticize the government as an administration;
we are less free in criticizing it as an institution. No one—not
even scientists—rises up in arms when technology is blamed;
but institutions command veneration, and one does not lightly
take their names in vain.

The only basis for blaming technology is that technology
changes while institutions lag. The ascription of blame, therefore, reflects an assumption that the natural condition of man
is static. It indicates a tendency to distrust change and to locate

security in sameness. This is the bias which has made equilibrium the central concept of social studies—the optimum state being thought of as equilibrium, while disequilibrium is considered an unnatural and temporary deviation. The same logic would have us believe that institutions are natural, and that technology is the trouble-maker. But there is no priority here; for man began to make tools as early as he began to make myths. Sameness and change are equally intrinsic to the human condition.

Identity is founded on value. It is founded, specifically, on those values which are at the top of the hierarchy—the beliefs, faiths, and ideals which integrate and determine subordinate values. These organizing values are, as has been described, institutional in nature, and so are vulnerable to the attrition and, sometimes, to the shock of the instrumental process. It is becoming increasingly difficult to maintain a firm sense of identity on the basis of these values; for their life-expectancy has decreased, and is continuing to decrease with a deceleration that is reciprocal to the acceleration of the instrumental process.

The development which runs from mores and institutions to values to goals to action and to identity has been undermined at its source. The confusion of values, the lack of goals, and the problem of identity are reflections of this trouble at the source. This is the crisis of our time as seen and approached from the vantage point of psychology. This is the same problem that other disciplines reach along quite different avenues. This is the trouble that disturbed the mores sleep of medieval

Europe, that became acute with the industrial revolution, and that has been erupting with increasing violence since 1914.

The stability of institutional values and of the mores from which they so largely derive has always been endangered from two sources: from without by contact with alien cultures; from within by the instrumental process. From both sources the impetus to change has so greatly increased as now to preclude stability. In the past it has been possible for a culture to decrease the danger from without by minimizing its contact with alien cultures. The integrity of Japanese customs was so insured for some hundreds of years. Technological advance has made such isolation progressively less feasible, and there is now no way of preventing the frequent and jarring clash of incompatible mores.

Even within the confines of a single culture the dynamic of technological change impacts with quickening blows on institutions, and constantly shortens the life-span of traditional ways. This is most particularly true of an industrial society where the rate of change is highest. Institutions have no authority except that they exist, and when the technological process makes their continued existence incompatible with the industrial arts, their death by attrition is underway.

It was scientific investigation that revealed the relativity of institutions and of mores, and nothing could be more obvious than that science provides a way out of mores nihilism. To lose our myths and gain the method of science is a net advantage. Yet curiously we feel more lost with the loss of our mores than heartened by the gain of a stronger ally. We sorrowfully dis-

card our immemorial beliefs, without developing much faith
in the method which alone was able to show them to us in a
clear light. We tend to regard science as just another of the
institutions of western civilization, as if it too were relative and
would pass. This view ignores a most important distinction:
institutions rest on tradition, vested authority, and ultimately
on force; science rests on experimental method. The findings
of science have general validity, are not contingent upon the
culture or tradition of the experimenter. The values, directives,
and judgments which issue from institutions have validity only
for those who happen to adhere to those institutions.

This view does not nominate science as an absolute to replace mores which are relative. Nothing is more true of science
than that it evolves. Its view of reality is subject to constant
revision. By its nature it progresses and changes, and a state of
final and complete knowledge is scientifically unthinkable.
Those who dream of absolute truth are experiencing a wish
that is relevant to institutions, not to science. Both are relative.
The issue is what they are relative to. The findings and assertions of science are always and necessarily incomplete, and are
relative to the state of scientific knowledge at any given time.
The findings and assertions of institutions are relative to the
culture that supports them.

It is doubtful if anyone has been put off from science by its
evolution. Nobody thinks of modern physics as unreliable because of the revisions it has effected in Newtonian mechanics.
The repudiation of past scientific knowledge is not the salient
feature of scientific progress. What is most characteristic is its
continuity, the progressive refining of insight, the cumulative

understanding. The state of scientific knowledge at any given time is all that we know. It makes no sense to disparage it simply because at some future time we will know more. Such as it is, it is the best we have, and is constantly getting better. It is the only source of assertions of rational warrant.

It must be something other than the relativity of scientific knowledge that puts us off. Science, it is said, can analyze a phenomenon, but cannot say whether it is good or bad. But good or bad for what? The attempt to know value without reference to purpose is an attempt to isolate experience from its context. All such inquiries of intrinsic value make reference, even if unwittingly, to an absolute, to a final destination. But if the question—good or bad for a specified purpose?—can be asked, then science can provide an answer or can admit ignorance. Often it must admit ignorance; and, since it cannot provide all the answers, we tend to forget what a very large number it does provide and the unique reliability that they possess.

The institutional solution to the value problem calls for the erection of a framework of belief that will remain stable while all else changes, that will provide a standard by which all things can be measured, a supreme value by which the value of everything else can be determined. But no value which is open to reconsideration and critical examination can be guaranteed to remain stable. Therefore, the proposed framework of belief must be secured against impulse and error by being placed beyond the realm of choice. It must be "for better or for worse, till death do us part." The evidence of history and of our own time speaks against such a proposal—not simply because it is not desirable, but because it is not possible.

It is sometimes suggested that the answer lies in the opposite direction, in making institutions more pliable. All institutions resist change, but some are more rigid than others. It is likely, for example, that American democracy is more flexible than was the old French monarchy. The Christian church must have a certain flexibility, or it could not have survived the stresses occasioned by Galileo, Luther, Darwin, and Freud. Without doubt a gain in flexibility may increase the life-span of an institution. But at times the instrumental process brings about situations which call, not for the modification, but for the abolition of an institution. This has happened to human sacrifice to gods, to slavery, and to countless other institutions. This is the rub in the proposal of greater institutional flexibility; for an institution can hardly be expected to be so flexible as to acquiesce to its own demise.

The instrumental solution calls for the elimination of all institutional coercions. Indeed, some instrumentalists seem to feel that the only good institutions are, like Indians, dead ones. But it is generally recognized now that when institutions are overthrown by force they are replaced, not by science, but by other institutions which may be more restrictive than those which were destroyed. Few persons, therefore, expect a scientific society to be established by revolution. But science, it is said, is winning the day, and may soon enable us to dispense altogether with myths and superstitions. This hope, too, is illusory. Man can give up his superstitions as soon as they are generally recognized as such, but there is no indication that

he will ever lose altogether the potentiality for creating superstitions in the guise of self-evident truth.

There is no solution to the value problem that will settle the
issue once and for all, no answer that will show the way to a
condition of man which is free of conflict. We must settle for
a path of progress, for progression as a process, for a direction
rather than an end. The path of progress is clear. It is given by
the instrumental process. It formulates no final goal; the mastery of one problem is followed simply by undertaking the
next. But it defines a path that leads away from humbug and
ignorance and exploitation and toward understanding, control,
and freedom.

Another world war may yet force a retreat into the past,
reinstating an older and more oppressive tyranny of institutions and mores. Unless we become too frightened we will not
voluntarily take such a course, but will continue further along
the path on which we have already come so far: giving up no
ground that has already been won, but extending the application of scientific method to areas thus far out of reach.

Modern man cannot recapture an identity out of the past;
for his old identity was not lost, but outgrown. Identity is not,
therefore, to be found; it is to be created and achieved.

{ THE VOCATIONAL
HAZARDS OF
PSYCHOANALYSIS

CAREER AND CONFLICT

For some persons the choice of a career issues easily from the various inner and outer circumstances of their lives which have a bearing on the matter. For others, divided within and driven to find a vocation which will resolve an inner conflict, the choice is made with difficulty and is not elective. Often not one but many conflicts are involved. The more numerous the conflicts the more difficult the choice becomes, and the less likely that any one career can resolve them all. The choice proves successful when the vocation makes possible a partial sublimated discharge of the impulses which are involved and a corresponding reduction in the warding-off activities of the ego.

It comes about at times, however, that the very conflict which has led one into a certain profession is aggravated by the practice of that profession. The vocation misleads. It proves to be different in practice from that which it was taken to be when viewed from the outside. The young man discovers only gradually that his vocation is not what he expected and, because of inner conflict, needed. A long time may elapse before he learns this, so long a time, in fact, that he may no longer be a young man, but at the mid-point of life and deeply committed. Indeed, he may never realize his mistake; for there are powerful forces opposed to such awareness if one has made certain crucial and irreversible decisions.

Many vocations are, in quality of experience, easily known: the nature of work in carpentry and chemistry, for example, may be correctly perceived by those whose acquaintance with these fields is relatively slight. There are a few vocations, however, which are truly knowable only after long experience. Those which mislead belong to this group. They have a quality which cannot be fully communicated in words. One has to find out for one's self. The most painful states of inner turmoil, the severest tests of integrity, arise in those professions which have these combined characteristics: of being truly knowable only from within; and of offering promise, when viewed from without, of alleviation of inner conflict—which promise is insidiously retracted by increasing proficiency in the field. Art is one such; the church is another; and, without implication that this completes the list, I suggest that psychoanalysis is a third.

Psychiatrists who have ministers as patients sometimes encounter personal undoing by professional experience and can retrospectively trace its development. The career decision of the minister is usually made in adolescence during the course of acute conflict of impulse with ego. This conflict is experienced as a struggle between good and evil and, other factors being propitious, eventuates in a call. The ministry offers unique advantages, the appeal of which is none the less strong by virtue of the advantages being perceived unconsciously. It offers partial vicarious gratification of impulse by bringing the minister into contact with evil in the sufferings of his parishioners. At the same time it promises to strengthen him against temptation. Religion having been, for him, the most effective curb on impulse, the active work of a minister may be expected to strengthen this curb. He will identify himself with the church, become the agent of God, assist others in combating evil in themselves, and so will gain added assurance of retaining control over the evil in himself. Such is the array of unconscious forces at the time of decision. For some persons this works out as planned; for others, for the hypothetical clergyman under consideration, the vocation belies its promise and matters gradually go awry.

His first parish experience is an eye-opener, an education more liberal by far than that offered by the seminary. Dealing with all manner of people in all kinds of circumstances, he finds that moral issues are insistently and perversely ambiguous. The line between good and evil will not stay clear. Black will not stay black, nor white white. He is puzzled and disturbed by the fog that settles over the once clear moral landscape. Being of a contemplative nature, his attempt to regain lost certainty takes the form, not only of prayer, but of further study and reflection. And, fortunately or diabolically, his profession provides ample time for just that. Over the course of years, along with exegetics and hermeneutics, he may also read Sumner and Dewey and Veblen and Russell; and rather than quelling his doubts, his reading feeds them. It comes about in time that he feels incompetent even to define such basic terms as right and wrong.

He may, of course, at any point in this development, call a halt. He may simply refuse to see anything further that is new and disturbing, and retreat with intransigent blindness into the nearest orthodoxy. Thereafter he will see black where he needs to see black, and white where he needs to see white. Intellectually and emotionally his development will have ended—the usual price of certainty. This may happen to any of us; many, indeed, who disdain such a solution will yet arrive at the same end, and quite totally without awareness. Psychoanalysts frequently describe one or another of their colleagues as rigid and dogmatic and authoritarian; yet no analyst ever so describes himself. The inescapable inference is that some of us have taken refuge in dogma without knowing that we have done so.

If the clergyman remains intellectually and emotionally open, his work may provide him with such insight as will force him eventually to relinquish belief in a personal God, in life after death, and in other of the absolutes which had guaranteed his security. In short, the very nature of his professional labors may undermine and finally destroy precisely those aspects of his profession which, by promising resolution of inner conflict, had drawn him into the profession in the first place. Sublimation may be lost and repression may fail, the old conflict erupting into consciousness. But it is no longer a conflict simply of impulse with ego. The minister is not now an adolescent, but a middle-aged man; and when he finds himself affirming from the pulpit propositions in which he no longer believes, he is faced with the loss of integrity and the onset of despair. What had seemed a stable adjustment has begun to crumble. Whether or not he can survey the damage, salvage those elements which are sound, and build a new structure of belief depends upon the courage, tenacity, and creative ability which he can mobilize to meet the crisis.

The experience of this minister is exactly analogous to developments in the lives of some psychoanalysts. These are the developments to be described here. The inner conflicts which lead certain persons to become analysts, the resolution of these conflicts which the profession seems to offer, the vicissitudes of the conflicting forces, the undermining and eventual destruction of the resolution—these are the issues to be examined. This account does not profile a typical psychoanalyst. The conflicts dealt with do not survey his psychology, nor even the determinants of his vocational choice. Those conflicts which achieve stable resolution in the practice of analysis are not here studied. Under scrutiny are only those inner conflicts which, for some persons, lead to the career choice of psychoanalysis and which are eventually aggravated by practice in this field.

For some persons the principal determinant of the vocational choice of psychoanalysis is to be found in the development of the capacity for insight and in the function of insight in the struggle for self-mastery. The capacity for insight is to be distinguished from any particular instance of insight, just as problem-solving ability is distinguishable from the solution to any one problem. It consists in the ability to look into obscure aspects of one's personality, to recognize disguised motivations, to integrate what is discovered with various elements of conscious experience, and to utilize one's findings in such a way as to bring about a change in feeling, action, and reaction. It implies a belief that no inner danger is so bad but that knowing about it will be better than not knowing. It presupposes, further, an implicit faith in the adaptive potential of intelligence, and the wish to place at the disposal of intelligence all available information.

When there occurs a high development of the capacity for insight, when the individual comes to depend on insight as the most reliable instrument for self-mastery, and when, nevertheless, inner conflict continues with dangerous intensity and precarious balance—when all of these conditions obtain they comprise a situation which, other factors being propitious, may determine the choice of psychoanalysis as a vocation. The following episode illustrates such a state of affairs at an early, but crucial, point in the development of the capacity for insight.

IMPASSE

Larry was nineteen years old—tall, pale, thin, withdrawn in manner, and often defensively arrogant. He had for some months been engaged in writing a novel which was to embody his ideas about love, the most remarkable of which was that physical love brings about the death of spiritual love, that if lovers would only love continently their love would last forever. That his personal experience had been only with the spiritual kind did not, as he saw it, disqualify him for this task.

In order to write this novel he had dropped out of college at the end of his second year. His mother, who now lived in Leeville, objected, but he had overridden her misgivings. Wanting to be alone, he had returned to San Antonio and there lived meagerly on the small allowance his mother sent him. He stayed in the Y.M.C.A., surrounded by many lonesome men, but made no friends. Occasionally he allowed himself a game of chess in the lobby, but for the most part was alone in his narrow room on the fourth floor. Living in a multitude, his life was separate and untouched.

Throughout the fall and winter he worked steadily, ten to twelve hours a day, seven days a week. Page after page was covered with words, his two dozen pencils wore down to stubs, and the manuscript increased in bulk and weight. In the late spring he became uncertain of the novel's worth. He continued to work as before, but the inspiration was gone and the work was drudgery. He was caught in a morass of words. He wrote, rewrote, revised, and re-revised, but working over brought no improvement. It was as though he were struggling with something that would not stay put. A chapter which one week he thought good would, when read the next, seem worthless. His mother's letters spoke more insistently of the necessity of his returning to college and of her inability to support him further in so uncertain a career as writing. Often she asked when the novel would be finished, but obviously looked forward to its completion, not as a significant accomplishment, but as the end of a whim in which she had indulged him. There remained to be written only the two final chapters. Unwilling to write them, however, while the value of those that preceded was in doubt, he had bogged down in the apparently endless task of revision. It was May, and his time was running out.

One night, after having worked for thirteen hours, he went to bed at two in the morning, but did not sleep. At five, attributing his insomnia to coffee, he got up and read. At eight he went down to the cafeteria for breakfast. The morning passed quietly and profitlessly. Between ten-thirty and twelve he dozed in his chair. After lunch, having bolstered himself with more coffee, he bathed and prepared for work. The wakefulness felt under a cold shower did not persist; the energy generated by caffeine did not lend itself to sustained effort; and after a while he gave it up. With a sense of guilt at not working, he waited as the day passed. From his window he watched the heat and glare of afternoon change to dusk and finally to cool darkness. At ten he went to bed, and at twelve was up again. While others slept, he went out in the city, drank coffee, and returned to his room. He forced himself to work, but for every sentence written a half hour was spent dawdling. His mind would at one moment be empty, at the next full of irrelevant ideas. At five he surveyed his production and knew that the night, too, had been wasted. He went to bed and again could not sleep, and at seven rose to the dreary prospect of another day.

The morning was spent in one of the plush chairs in the lobby, dozing now and then. On arousing himself in the afternoon, he felt stuporous, his limbs stiff. After another futile attempt he laid his writing aside, pondered the matter, decided that exercise might help, and set out immediately on a long walk. Reaching the suburbs, he spent an hour alternately running and walking, in order that the exercise would be sufficiently strenuous. Upon returning, he was thirsty and exhausted. After a hot shower he went to the cafeteria, but discovered he was not hungry. His only craving was for something cold. He could not recall ever having been so tired. Confident that he would sleep twelve hours, he went to bed early. Two hours later he was still awake.

It occurred to him that he was trying too hard, that his fear of not sleeping was keeping him awake. He was afraid that he couldn't work if he didn't sleep, and he had to work. He tried to make his mind a blank. The void was quickly filled with sexual imagery. Presently, in disgust, he got up and began to read a book on the technique of fiction. With the subsidence of desire, weariness returned. At three he went back to bed and counted sheep, but this didn't help. At five he slept, but woke in fright an hour later from a bad dream. He was relieved at the knowledge of having slept, and thought he would simply roll over and drop off again. But something prodded at his mind, unkindly, insistently. His novel . . . . Could he ever straighten the thing out? Make it right? If he did not sleep he would never be able to finish it. It occurred to him that the street light shining through the window might be keeping him awake. He lowered the blind and tied a handkerchief around his head. Again he was besieged with sexual imagery, and got up.

During the morning he gave thought to his insomnia and

decided it was due to overwork. In no position to prescribe an extended rest cure, he allowed himself only the remainder of that day for relaxation. During that time he resolved not to think about his writing. In the afternoon he played ping pong and chess. At dinner he was vaguely disturbed by his inability to eat. In the evening he went to a movie alone. These things did not help, and for another night he remained awake. In the early morning he tried a method which had been recommended by the room clerk. It consisted of counting slowly, opening and closing one's eyes with each count. "You'll never reach thirty," the clerk had guaranteed. He was wrong. At one hundred his fatigue was extreme, and at two hundred he could no longer move his eyelids. But he could still count, and his mind was wakeful. A fit of coughing led him to wonder if he might be developing tuberculosis.

The following morning he went to see a general practitioner. The doctor performed a cursory physical examination, gave him a sedative, said there was no reason why he should not sleep, and advised exercise. His tonsils, the doctor said, were infected and, if the insomnia continued, should be removed. Though his fatigue was already extreme, Larry spent the afternoon and evening in the Y.M.C.A. pool. Too tired for sustained effort, he would swim the length of the pool and back, rest a minute, and repeat the process. At nine in the evening he prepared for bed and swallowed the one capsule he had been given. Almost immediately he felt dizzy and sleep came effortlessly. At two in the morning he woke, and, though the effect of the drug was still appreciable, did not sleep again that night.

When daylight came he sat in the lobby by a window, looking out on the street. Repeatedly he tried to think through
his problem, to discover the cause. His eyes burned, his head
ached, and he was weak and tremulous. Whatever the hypothesis to be examined, his thought would falter and change
to daydreams. A girl walked by, a pretty girl, her heels click-
ing on the sidewalk. He watched her idly. As she passed from
his view at the end of the block, she reappeared immediately
on the stage of his mind—without clothes. It occurred to him
that sexual continence might have produced in him an endo-
crine imbalance and that this, in turn, was causing insomnia.
For some two hours he considered the possibility of sexual
intercourse as a form of therapy, his state of mind alternating
between feverish excitement and abysmal guilt. Eventually
he gave in to desire. He felt that his life was falling to pieces
and that the act would make no difference. At twelve noon,
feeling himself a scoundrel, a sinner, and a fool, he left the
Young Men's Christian Association for his first experience of
what, in his novel, he called "carnal love." The prostitute was
a silent, dull-witted Mexican girl, the heat was stifling, the
circumstances were sordid, and the price was cheap.

An hour later, back in the Y.M.C.A. lobby, he sat down
to analyze the experience, but found that there was little to
think about, nothing to conclude. After a while he went up-
stairs to his room and lay on his bed. Still he could not sleep.
Too nervous to lie still, he returned to the lobby and spent the
afternoon playing chess. At times he could forget that he was
dangling, but not for long. His fatigue reminded him that he
was avoiding a problem to the solution of which chess would

in no way contribute. At six, having eaten nothing during the day, he felt hungry and went to the cafeteria, but with the first mouthful was satisfied. In the evening he tried to read, but his attention wandered. Too exhausted to write, he went to a movie, again with the feeling that he was running away from something.

That night he stood for a long time in a hot shower before retiring, while through his mind there ran a refrain: "I've got to sleep. I've got to sleep. If I can't sleep I can't work. I've got to sleep." But necessity was not soporific. At midnight he got up and tried to read, but drifted off into daydreams. At two o'clock he lay down again, telling himself that he did not care whether he slept or not; but indifference was of no more avail than determination. Images of violence came to mind: he saw himself striking, slashing, piercing—machine-gunning a multitude in a narrow street. Four o'clock found him still awake. Too much on edge to stay in bed, he dressed and went for a walk. In contrast to his vigorous exercising of four days ago, he now walked slowly. With only slight exertion his heart beat painfully, giving him a sense of threatened suffocation.

Never had the city seemed so deserted or lonely as it did now in the gray light. For blocks no person could be seen. The only vehicles were an occasional cab or milk wagon. A surprising number of cats loitered aloofly in the closed entrances of shops, arching their backs against unfriendly doors, mewing as he passed, and waiting unhappily for shopkeepers to open their stores. There was a faint, cool mist in the air which softened the outlines of buildings and obscured some of the dirt and stains of the city. After a while he stopped on a corner to watch the sunrise. Across the street was a hospital, from one of the windows of which a nurse looked out at him for a moment, then disappeared. He could hear the sounds of breakfast being prepared. He drifted off into a pleasant fantasy of being a doctor, bending over a hospital bed, listening to the heart of a critically ill child.

Returning to the Y.M.C.A., he went to the coffee shop for breakfast, but the smell of doughnuts and eggs repelled him. He ordered only coffee, and on lifting the cup was surprised at the tremor of his hand. Drinking in sips, he sat there in a daze. After a while, as the taste of sugar and cream impregnated the mucous in the back of his throat, he became nauseated. On reaching the toilet he vomited. Feeling weak and sick, he slowly mounted the four flights of steps to his room. His eyes stung. Looking in the mirror, he saw that they were bloodshot and sunken. His face was haggard. His trousers hung loosely about his hips.

Sitting on the edge of the bed, he wondered how long this ordeal had been going on. Six days, he discovered on counting back. The information lay inertly in his mind. He felt capable of neither reason nor feeling. The refrain, "I've got to sleep. If I can't sleep I can't work," ran round his mind. Too tired to undress, he lay down fully clothed, but could not lie still. It was as though something were forcing him to twist and turn and roll, making of the attempt to sleep an agony of restlessness. After a few minutes, unable to endure it any longer, he got up and sat at his desk.

It was eight o'clock. Another day was beginning. A day which gave every promise of being like the last. A day of nausea, nervousness, and paralyzing fatigue, of chess and movies and cheap magazines, a day which would end at last in a night like the one just finished. Suddenly his despair changed to desperation.

He bit his lip and struck the table with his fist. Repeatedly, slowly, he pounded the table in rhythmic fury. The muscles of his back contracted. His head was drawn back, his feet pressed hard against the wall, his chest constricted. It occurred to him that he was going to have a convulsion. Obscurely he felt that he was acting, and that he could stop it, but was not sure he wanted to. One of the blows missed the table top, his knuckles grazing the edge. With the pain he regained control of himself, and after a moment was able to relax. He extended his fingers, watched drops of blood stand out on the abrasions, and realized that he had reached an extremity of trouble. He turned his mind once more to the problem. Each day he had done this, and each day had failed. As the problem had become more serious, his ability to deal with it had diminished. Now the need was urgent. There would be few more opportunities.

He considered, but rejected, the idea of going to see the doctor again. Since exercise had failed, the tonsillectomy would now be recommended. He returned insistently to the thought that there must be some explanation, that a person just doesn't stop sleeping without reason. Now, for the first time, he wondered if there were something wrong with his mind. He considered this unlikely, but decided to investigate it anyway. After washing his face and bandaging his hand, he set out for the public library.

At the card catalogue he looked under the heading of "Sleep," where he found nothing more pertinent than *The Sleeping Beauty*. Then he located a textbook of general psychology and studied it for about an hour, finding it to be a compartmentalized discussion of perception, memory, imagination, and intelligence. Nothing in it touched on his problem. Consulting the card catalogue again, he located a book on physiology. This turned out to be a ponderous volume, in the index of which he found a reference to sleep. With frequent use of the dictionary, he labored through several pages of learned discourse about the hypothalamus, water balance, acid metabolites, and the like, deciding finally that the author was not only unable to explain sleep, but was equally at a loss as to why people stay awake. He knew of no other likely works to consult.

It was on his way out of the library that, quite by chance, he found what he needed. In the foyer was a shelf of new books, among them one titled *Understanding Human Nature*, by Alfred Adler. Leaning against the wall, he read the introduction, and then read further. Presently he returned to the reading room with it and soon was engrossed. He spent the day with this book, pausing every now and then to reflect on what he had read, to apply it to himself, and to examine the result.

At the end of the day he had his answer. He had, he decided, known for some weeks that his novel was of no merit, but had concealed this information from himself. As the awareness of failure became more difficult to avoid, the insomnia had provided a symptomatic defense for his self-esteem. If he couldn't sleep he couldn't work; if he couldn't work he couldn't finish the novel; if he could not finish the novel, then no one would be able to say definitely that it was a failure.

That evening he wrote and mailed a letter to his mother telling her that he had misjudged himself, that he did not at present have the ability to write a good novel, and that he intended to return to college as soon as possible.

At seven o'clock he turned back the covers on his bed. The linen had been changed that day; and the sight and feel and smell of the starched sheets, the wonderful softness and resiliency of the mattress, had a unique quality of goodness. He fell asleep at once and did not wake until late the following afternoon.

INSIGHT

This incident illustrates several relevant aspects of the conflict under consideration. In the struggle within Larry between impulse and ego, the ego's control was precarious. His writing took place entirely within the sphere of this conflict, the choice of writing having been determined by a need to augment the ego's slight preponderance of power. The content of the novel was designed to strengthen his suppression of sexual and aggressive drives by elaborating a fear of impulse into a philosophy of life. Since writing is a solitary activity, it was meant, also, to spare him that intensification of drive which is consequent to proximity to people. And the writing of fiction provided, for his narcissistic needs, a basis for anticipations of fame. Even these weighty vocational supports failed, however, to establish a clear margin of safety; they provided at best only a fragile balance of power.

It may be assumed that he could have avoided the crisis had he managed to write a good novel, but this proposition is as empty as it is true. Creative activity, while always a product of conflict, necessarily fails when, as in this case, it is wholly committed in an intrapsychic struggle. For in these circumstances the urgency of the personal problem defines the vantage point of the creator, thereby precluding the achievement of a work of general validity. The more desperate the personal need the less the likelihood of creative success. Comparable situations occur, though rarely, among psychoanalysts. If an analyst needs to succeed with a certain case in order to avoid a personal breakdown, the urgency of his need is likely to vitiate his work. For the conduct of a successful analysis, like the creation of a good novel, calls for a considerable segment of ego-functioning to be conflict-free.

As Larry's creative activity began to fail, the ego's slight preponderance of power was lost. The symptom of insomnia was clearly an emergency defense. He simply could not risk falling asleep. Even his clock-round vigilance did not suffice; a sexual impulse broke through and was acted upon in a manner which could not be integrated in his life. At this point the neurosis was clearly unstable. The insomnia could not hold for long. Barring some intervention, his illness could have been expected to progress quickly to a more stable symptomatic form—possibly tuberculosis, his father's illness, which he had already begun to consider in fantasy.

The insight, by facilitating a shift in defensive measures, enabled him to avoid this development. The conflicting forces were so evenly matched that it was essential for him to be engaged in an activity which would augment ego resources and so provide a margin of safety. The insight was so formulated as to enable him to abandon creative writing—which had been undertaken with this in mind, but had failed—and to begin something new, which might succeed. The intellectual pleasure which accompanied the insight, the sense of mastery at having penetrated a mystery, enabled him to make the switch without overwhelming loss of self-esteem.

The particular formulation which he achieved is not remarkable. He might have read some other book and arrived at a quite different, but equally helpful, understanding. It may be remarked in passing, however, that it was his good fortune not to have picked up a book of Freud's; for the information he would have there encountered, being further removed from conscious experience, could not have been utilized. Adler's book, dealing with neurotic conflict in more accessible terms, functioned for him in the manner of a good interpretation: it extended but slightly the area of the known.

Far more significant than the content of his insight was the use to which it was put. Insight is an edged tool, can cut through neurotic formations. But it is not automatic; it is, as it were, a hand tool. Having discovered the cutting edge and gotten the feel of the instrument, Larry performed the indicated operation. The experience was an active one. Incidentally, one handles such a tool more deftly if, as in this case, one has had some part in its forging. Insight received prefabricated may help with a present problem, but provides no continuing security. Problems change and there is no end to them; and if one is ever to be independent of professional insight-makers one needs, not specific solutions, but the capacity for creating them as occasion requires.

Larry's insight occurred at a time of bad trouble. Such an experience, if it proves repeatable, will have far-reaching effects. He will come to rely on insight as on nothing else. So far as personal security is concerned, he will value it above friends, fame, love, or money. It is something of which no chance can deprive him. It is utterly reliable. In Larry's case the capacity for insight developed over the course of years, and alleviated inner conflict to a moderate degree. He was able to maintain the upper hand over repressed drives and suffered no further symptoms, but never achieved serenity. He continued to be driven to find a vocation which would, as he hoped, solve this conflict once and for all.

The situation which has been described is, for some persons—as, some fifteen years later, it proved to be for Larry—the principal determinant of the vocational choice of psychoanalysis. In the expectations of the young man making this choice, insight is to be enormously extended, with commensurately improved control over inner danger. Forbidden impulses are to obtain vicarious release, with corresponding reduction in pressure from within. One will become a healer, will free gifted but impotent people from neurotic chains, with result-

ing gratification of narcissistic needs. In these ways the practice of psychoanalysis is expected to replace inner conflict
with lasting peace. It is but slowly that the young man learns
that he has misjudged the field, that the promise which had
seemingly been extended is not going to be honored.

For a while all goes well. As a psychiatric resident he begins
his acquaintance with an absorbing body of scientific literature
and has the fascinating experience of inquiring into the more
private and guarded aspects of people's lives. As a psycho-
therapist he has few successes, and his cures are followed by
relapses; but he is not discouraged. Therapeutic failure has,
rather, the effect of orienting him more strongly toward psychoanalysis. "One must not," he reflects, "expect too much
from psychotherapy. It is at best a hit or miss affair: too many
variables . . . infrequent appointments . . . no chance to
work out the transference." His faith in insight is unshaken,
and without misgivings he parts company with those of his
colleagues who take up the physical and pharmaceutical therapies. He is likely, indeed, to express some scorn for their syr-
inges and shock-boxes. As for himself, he applies to the Institute.

In the course of several years of didactic training in psychoanalysis he learns much that is useful clinically and is exposed
to a great deal of theory the usefulness of which is not so apparent. If his luck is average he will have, in equal measure,
good teachers and bad—those who encourage the development of his capacity for independent thought, and those who
require that he simply accept the information which they
have to instill. If he is insecure and passive, he is apt to esteem

more highly the authoritarian teachers; for they provide him with rules. If he has the freedom to be skeptical, he will be irritated by dogmatic instruction and will be chagrined to observe that, whereas societies of biologists and chemists easily accommodate exponents of contradictory hypotheses, societies of psychoanalysts are split by such differences.

As his personal analysis nears completion he feels somewhat disappointed. The radical character change he had hoped for has not been realized, and he still has anxiety in the same old circumstances. Some of his more troublesome rigidities have been loosened, however, and he is more secure. One should not, he reasons, expect from the training analysis of a candidate the same result as from the therapeutic analysis of a hysteric.

Uncomplicated cases of hysteria prove to be rare, however; and, after waiting several months, he begins supervised analyses of an unhappy artist with hypertension and an impossible marriage, and of a young woman who has had to drop out of college because of continually washing her hands. His efforts with these patients, over the course of several years, are not altogether successful: the artist proves to have strong psychopathic tendencies and a weak ego; the girl with the hand-washing compulsion is found to be schizophrenic. He has nevertheless displayed reasonable skill, has profited from instruction, and in due time—that is, six or seven years after beginning his training—he is graduated.

At no time during this period has his experience of psychoanalysis, either as patient or therapist, matched his expectations; but it has always been possible to rationalize the discrepancy. As a full-fledged analyst, his experience continues to fall short of his expectations. In his search for a way to close the gap he now falls under the influence of various schools, with corresponding modifications in his technique. Some of these help with certain patients, but none of them provides him with a conviction of professional competence. In the early stages of his career he emphasizes the correct formulation. As this fails to effect a change, he concentrates more on "working through." With repeated failure, he decides that the trouble lies in the fact that the insight has not been emotionally experienced. He limits his interpretations more carefully to the area of experienced feeling. Later he may conclude that interpretations of content cannot be mutative, and that he should interpret only in the transference. Nothing works really well. He still cannot rest secure in the practice of a method which yields predictable results with dependable regularity. A time comes, eventually, when his doubts can no longer be parried. They make themselves heard and felt, and a period of disillusionment ensues.

The disillusionment is a function of the differing ways in which insight, as a means to self-mastery, enters the experience of analyst and patient. Analysts are purveyors of insight; patients are applicants for magic. The original relationship, of which the transference is a later edition, is one of child to parent, and hence is characterized by an enormous discrepancy in size, power, wisdom, and ability to protect, punish, and gratify. When the child becomes an adult, and an analysand, there exists between him and his analyst a difference of far less magnitude. But in the transference the original discrepancy is recreated; and the patient, accordingly, expects, not the modest help of insight, but the abolition of fears by parental edict and the gratification of needs out of the goodness of parental heart. Insofar, therefore, as patients experience transference feelings, they are expecting magical performance, either good or bad. And since analysis establishes optimal conditions for the development of transference, the expectation of magic is extreme.

In perhaps no other vocation is one so continuously the object of such intense transference feelings. Ministers are expected to work wonders, but can displace part of the burden to God, maintaining that the power is His, that His ways are inscrutable, and that the minister functions only as agent. Those in positions of public power are expected to perform miracles, but are surrounded by administrative assistants, protected by protocol, and so are spared much of the direct impact of transference. The analyst is not so buffered. He cannot expect his secretary to mollify the patient who has come to hate him, nor call on God to extricate him from a transference impasse. There are only two persons in the consulting room and the analyst has been tagged. He's "it," and must handle as best he can a demand for magical performance that continues —fearful, angry, trusting, or frantic—hour after hour, day after day.

This is a position for which he is, in temperament, poorly qualified. For he is not inclined to the exertion of occult influence. His orientation is not superstitious, but matter-of-fact. Ritual and incantation are alien to him. Faced with a mystery, he does not invoke the supernatural, but admits ignorance. His approach to a problem is to gather the evidence and to subject it to scrutiny. He relies on reason rather than faith. He is characterized by taking pains. He is, it is true, a person who has elected to work with phenomena which are among the most puzzling in human experience, but his intent is not to exploit mystery but to unravel it. And, having solved a mystery, he is not inclined to keep the solution to himself as a source of personal power, but to convey his understanding as fully as possible to his patient. Actors, politicians, evangelists, and gamblers might be expected to possess in considerable measure the propensity to use magic; psychoanalysts, it may be surmised, possess this trait to even a lesser degree than do other scientists. For, while it is not rare for a physicist to be superstitious about the inner life of man, it is exceedingly rare for a psychoanalyst to be superstitious about crystal structure or the behavior of molecules. The psychoanalyst is one who maintains that even that area of experience which is least accessible to scientific investigation is as strictly determined and as fully subject to natural law as any other, and that it is properly approached with the same matter-of-fact attitude with which a biologist examines the nature of a virus.

It comes about, therefore, that the analyst—he who, of all people, is least disposed to use magic—becomes the object of the most intense and continuous demand for magical performance. Theoretically he is prepared for this: the analyst does not gratify transference, does not manipulate transference, does not offer emotional placebos; he analyzes. In practice, however, it frequently is impossible to substitute the uses of reason for the demand for magic.

The disillusionment of the analyst begins, therefore, with

his awareness of the limited efficacy of insight. Many of his patients can achieve correct dynamic formulations, but are unable to act accordingly. For them, insight is more a subject of discussion than an instrument of change. Other of his patients are prone enough to action, but act impulsively and without understanding. The capacity for verbal formulations of the unconscious is common; the capacity for action is common; but the capacity to combine understanding and action in such a way as to alter character according to plan is rare. Slowly he is forced to the realization that insight is not for his patients the edged tool that it is for him.

The subtle and complex structure of psychoanalysis as a therapeutic science rests upon a conviction of the value of insight. Resistance, working through, emotional insight, interpretation within the transference—these concepts denote essential aspects of technique, but do not replace insight. They bespeak, rather, the means by which insight is to be made effective. As the young analyst loses belief in the mutative potency of insight, the foundation of psychoanalysis is, in his view, weakened, and the edifice becomes unstable. The psychoanalytic theory of therapy is readily accepted by the student; it hangs together in a more or less coherent system. But its validity is contingent upon the efficacy of the therapeutic method which derives from it. In analysis, he has been taught, the pathogenic conflicts are re-experienced in a regressive transference neurosis; interpretations are made within the transference; the material is worked through; the conflicts are resolved; and there results a structural alteration of the personality, a radical character change. So exact is this account that it might have been carved in stone. Nothing of such precision and finality occurs in his office. With his interpretations he writes in water. His patients get better and get worse. Most of them derive some benefit from his efforts, but of structural alterations and radical character changes he sees little. He is forced reluctantly toward the conclusion that psychoanalysis is not what it is represented to be, and he begins to be troubled by a vague sense of fraudulence.

This is a crucial time in his professional life. From this point onward his development may take any one of several courses. None of them will be easy. Each will involve pain or loss. They are the vocational hazards to which he is exposed by virtue of the conflict which made him a psychoanalyst. In the soil of his chosen vocation the conflict has been transformed and now bears strange fruit.

Of those courses open to him the least painful is a retreat into dogma. If he takes this path, the cancerous doubts which threaten his vested professional interest are abolished by fiat. A vital relation between theory and practice is one of mobile interaction, each exerting an effect on the other. It calls for skepticism, freedom of inquiry, and tolerance of doubt. It presupposes the freedom to revise theory in the light of experience, and the intuition to look for undiscovered aspects of reality because of the implications of theory. This is lost by him who takes refuge in dogma. Henceforth the criterion of truth is not experience, but the book. The sanctity of psychoanalytic theory and technique is maintained, but at the cost of severing its connection with clinically observed events. As he sees it, his experience matches his theory quite closely; but the matching takes place in his own mind. He simply sees black where he needs to see black, and white where he needs to see white. Once one gets the knack of it, the technique is easy. Such concepts as resistance, negative therapeutic reaction, and psychotic ego lend themselves readily to intellectual legerdermain. Many analysts become true virtuosos at this game; but even the novice can, if diligent, accommodate his clinical experience to existing theory. Such a development marks the end of the analyst as a creative scientist. He has become a true believer. In losing his doubts he has lost his open mind. He may study for the rest of his life, he may write many papers; but the maps he draws will be tracings. The paths through new territory will be cut by others.

Some analysts who take refuge in dogma become the serious and able defenders of orthodoxy. They are constantly busy maintaining and decorating the house that Freud built, and they openly and honestly oppose anyone bent on remodeling. They may be arch-conservatives, but they have integrity; and what they profess, they believe. Others who make of their science a creed are less successful. They achieve but an uneasy suppression of doubt, and remain divided within. Covertly the doubt spreads. They believe neither in the value of their work nor in the validity of their concepts, but gloss over their disbelief, pretending all is well. Because they do not openly face their misgivings, they suffer an insidious undermining of integrity. They are reactionary in the extreme; yet they defend nothing. They don't study, they don't write, and hence cannot ably support orthodox theory. Their hostility for innovators is virulent, but takes the form of snide comment rather than scholarly refutation. They attack out of fear of the new rather than conviction in the old. They speak in tones of outrage of this or that analyst who has tampered with the libido theory, yet could not themselves define this theory. And were it stated for them, they would not know—if they could be honest—whether they believed it or not.

There are, however, analysts who, at the cost of deepening inner conflict, maintain an open mind and persist in evaluating theory and technique in the light of clinical observation. Their experience is one of progressive discouragement and spreading skepticism. It seems to them that they accomplish nothing of lasting value. Even when a cure is effected they cannot with confidence take credit, but feel that the result may be supposed with equal plausibility to have derived from an intercurrent development in the course of analysis. At times they regard themselves with distaste as highly skilled and overpaid professional comforters. Their experience and their skepticism transform the principles of psychoanalysis into conjectures, which one by one are jettisoned. The more rigid technical rules are the first to go, followed by the more sophisticated principles. Structural concepts are seen as anthropomorphisms. The economic point of view becomes an absurd aping of precise science. The use of one's own unconscious as a tool becomes the rationalization of autistic reverie. As Descartes' searching skepticism deprived him, one by one, of all of the philosophical principles in which he had formerly believed, leaving him finally bereft of all but one affirmation, "I think, therefore I exist," so the analyst may, by the mediocrity of his therapeutic results, be led to discard the tenets on which his professional life is founded, and be left, finally, with a belief only in the significance of unconscious motivation to neurotic misery. Sometimes even this is lost.

Goaded by the falling value of his intellectual stock, he may make of his doubts a counterdogma and become a professional dissident, expending his creative potential in attacks on the orthodox. If unusually gifted and skillful, he may have the good fortune to be expelled from the ranks and thereby achieve martyrdom. If but a run of the mill deviant, this honor will be denied him. He will simply be ignored, left in the rancorous position of being a rebel of whom no one is afraid.

If he does not take this way out, he will wish he were an internist, a physicist, or a farmer. Any honest work would be better than this. He will think about getting out. Such a change in life-direction is easily made in one's teens, but he is now in his forties and is deeply committed. The conflict in which he is engulfed is not simply the adolescent struggle of impulse with ego. The issue of integrity is involved. He knows that he is a complex person and suspects that any vocation would have presented him with comparable troubles. He cannot keep changing. Somewhere he must make a stand. The suffering of his patients is real; of this he has no doubt. Their need for help is real. His theory and technique may be phony, but the problem is not flimsy. The issues of neurosis are shadowy, but the adversary is formidable and the challenge is worthy.

He may have lost all of the tenets of his professional faith. At the nadir he may retain only the belief that it is possible for one person to help another. But from even this depth a comeback may be possible. It depends on his intelligence and creative ability; and it depends, also, on his courage, tenacity, and integrity. If he prevails, he will discover that much that he has discarded has value and can be salvaged. And when he takes up again some discarded element of technique or theory it will become more surely his own than it was at that prior time when he had accepted it so uncritically. Insight will never again appear to him as the irresistible instrument of personality change which once it seemed, but it will always be a useful tool to have near at hand. He may never achieve such comprehensive certainty as he had as a student. But this is all to the good. For if he insists on certainty, his skepticism will have been in vain; and he will achieve in the end—as did Descartes—a closed system of psychological absolutes which, though perhaps more acceptable to the temperament of the creator, embodies the worst faults of the system against which he rebelled. There is so much in experience that is contingent and mysterious that one has no business with a theory that strains at the absolute. A living science is more concerned with probing its unknowns than in praising its knowns, and he who cannot live with some fundamental uncertainties is not an investigator but a pilgrim.

INTIMACY

For some persons the problem of intimacy is the principal determinant of the vocational choice of psychoanalysis. The conflict is between the tendencies that lead to closeness, and the fear that is evoked by closeness. The actions prompted by loneliness, by longing, and by the needs of sex, love, friendship, and sharing are curtailed by an anxiety that can be allayed only by estrangement. If the needs are met, one is vulnerable; if security is maintained, one is frustrated. The needs are common to all; the anxiety is a product of individual experience.

Perhaps no one is entirely free of this conflict. Some persons —those under consideration here—are host to a particularly virulent strain. Since the needs are normal, it is some expression of defense which signalizes the presence of the conflict. Aloofness, detachment, and isolation are common indications. Great intensity of this conflict may exist, however, without visible sign. To all outward appearances a person may be intimately engaged with others; no one save himself—and one or two others who have made unusually persistent efforts to reach him —may know that he is surrounded by an invisible wall and cannot be touched.

When the conflict is severe it exerts a profound effect on all aspects of living, including the choice of vocation. Often it leads to one or another of the simply solitary occupations: in this event the vocation does not resolve the conflict, but rather consolidates the defense, providing a justification for continuing isolation. At times, however, it leads to a career which offers promise of resolution. Art is one such. As an artist, it is assumed, one will be able to retain in all aspects of daily living the isolation necessary for one's security; at the same time one will achieve, via one's creations, a profound intimacy in which the deepest feelings of many people will be touched by one's own, and will respond. So it must seem—dimly or quite unconsciously—to the young man who, for these reasons, is about to choose art as his life work.

The physician who is torn by this conflict and who elects to become a psychoanalyst is attempting a comparable solution. He will, it is assumed, achieve intimacy by hearing secrets none other can hear, not even a priest; for a priest cannot take so much time. He will enter hidden recesses of another life none other can enter; for no one else is possessed of such a sensitive technique. At the same time he will maintain the isolation he requires. Indeed, it seems to him that psychoanalysis not only permits but demands isolation. An analyst is not to become involved with his patients; very well, he will remain uninvolved. He will require his patients to lie down; he will sit, unseen, behind the couch. He will direct his patients to talk continuously; he will speak infrequently, and not on demand, but only at his own discretion. The conditions optimal for psychoanalysis appear to fit the conditions optimal for his personal security with a rare precision. A more fortunate concordance could hardly be imagined.

The inner conflict which propels him so insistently toward psychoanalysis does not, however, recommend him to those in charge of training. They consider it rather a handicap; and one of the functions of the preparatory analysis is to resolve this conflict, or, failing that, to steer him toward a field of endeavor in which it will be a less serious liability. It is common knowledge, however, that many candidates in whom this conflict has been only minimally alleviated nevertheless acquire the status of a fully qualified analyst. Many factors conspire to this end. The training analysis may extend over a period of four or five years. In the meantime the candidate has completed all of his didactic work and may be well into one or more supervised analyses. By this time his investment of money and effort and time is of such magnitude that his mentors may simply not have the heart to dismiss him. He is apt, moreover, to be unusually intelligent and articulate; for those who have not these advantages to offset their handicap seldom get even so far as this. And the uses of intelligence may effectively disguise the far-reaching consequences of his inner struggle. He may excel at theory, may thread his way nimbly through the maze of conceptual subtleties. For these reasons many candidates who experience continuous inner struggle about the issue of intimacy do succeed in becoming analysts.

What, then, is the experience of such an analyst in his chosen field? He directs toward his patients certain unconscious attitudes and impulses which, were they put into words, would sound somewhat as follows.

"I am a technician of loneliness, but suffer from the malady I treat and spend my days alone, silent, listening. I am tormented by an ineludible yearning to lose myself in the inner life of another. And yet I never dare.

"But I am devious, I am clever. I find ways. My need lies unseen behind a mask of calm understanding. My synapses click briskly, indefatigably, with unutterable dryness. I keep trying. I find ways. I have found a way to make others—others who suffer—come close to me.

" '*Tell me your thoughts.*'

"Speak to me. Say all that occurs to you, at whatever cost in shame. Nothing is irrelevant. Everything is important. I want to know everything—every last ghost of thought or impulse—

that flickers across your consciousness for however brief a fragment of interminable time. I want to be close to someone, want to lose for a moment the crushing burden of my insuffer-able and isolate identity. But I can't open my heart and come close to you. I am afraid. And deep down, because I am afraid, I hate. I don't dare come close to you. You come close to me. Tell me whatever crosses your mind.

" 'Perhaps it is some thought of me that blocks you?' "

And what does cross their minds? They suffer, they fear, they bare their souls in torment. And what crosses their minds —and lips—is something to hear.

"No, by God, it does *not* mean that! Sometimes, perhaps, when I'm late it *may* mean I'm 'hostile,' but not always, and not today. And moreover, for your information, every time I happen to close my hand it does *not* mean I'm angry and have an unconscious impulse to strike you. And every time I chance to move my purse it does *not* indicate resentment at having to pay your fee. I'm sick to death of such guile. You can twist anything I say or do to mean whatever you want it to mean. And when you do this it's called 'interpretation'; when I do it, it's 'distortion of reality.'

"I'm fed up. A whole year I've been at this. A mixed-up, mired-down, miserable, wasted, Goddamned year. Two hun-dred hours of supine introspection. And for what? What have I got out of it? Nothing. Not a Goddamn thing. I'm twice as miserable as before. It doesn't help. Words . . . . 'Tell me your thoughts.' 'What are your feelings about that?' 'You seem hostile today.' Christ almighty, I don't need you to tell me I'm hostile. I'm not hostile, I'm mad as a bitch tiger, that's all. And one of these days I'm going to find the guts to walk out of here and not come back. And I hope dianetics takes over —dianetics or chiropractic or crystal-ball-gazing or tea-leaf-reading. They'd do as much as you and be a damn sight cheaper.

"You haven't helped me, and what's more I don't believe you help anyone. Who have you cured? Who the hell do you think you're fooling? Your damned analysis doesn't even enable a patient to adjust well to the poverty in which it leaves him. I could lie here forever, with you saying, 'Now you're feeling toward me as if I were your father.' It doesn't help. Words . . . . You do nothing. You're just a listener—a subtle, crafty listener. Year after year you listen. You keep your miserable patients in analysis so long that eventually something happens, something quite apart from analysis. And if this something is for the worse, the patient breaks off treatment. Then you're not to blame for the failure. He 'terminated treatment prematurely.' Hogwash. I suppose you didn't 'fully analyze his castration complex'! What the hell! How many years do you want? Who else hedges like that? Who else demands such odds before delivering the goods? Who the hell do you think you are anyway?

"Or else something happens for the better. The patient—or somebody, for Christ's sake—gets hold of his bootstraps and yanks. Then you can say you *did* 'analyze the castration complex,' 'working through' is complete, and the analysis a 'success.' If I were you I'd cry in shame.

"How can you be in this business so long and still not see

you change no one, cure no one? Or maybe you *do* know—know and proceed cynically, raking in the money, spending your weekends in Bermuda, too gutless to admit you're selling fake merchandise, using the confusion of the desperately miserable to maintain a lucrative racket. Stealing pencils from the blind would be more honorable!

"I'll tell you why I was late today! Two blocks from your office a crowd gathered. An old man had fallen on the street. A skinny, filthy wreck of a man. He was carrying a bag of potatoes, and they scattered over the sidewalk. Everybody stared. One lady sniffed, 'These drunks!' and tilted her snobbish nose a little higher. Well, I picked up his Goddamn potatoes and put them back in the sack, and stayed with him till he could get up and walk.

"But you wouldn't understand that. You wouldn't soil your lily white hands on anything so vulgar. You would saunter on, murmuring a few clever interpretations. *You* wouldn't be late. You'd get back to this plush office right on time. I'm sick of your office—everything so tasteful, so expensive, so just right. Your waiting room so exquisitely furnished, so beautifully lighted. Just the right number of water colors by just the right artists. And none of these common magazines like *Life* or *Colliers*. Oh no! Just *Epoch* and *The Kenyon Review*. And it's all oh so discreet, with thick doors and trick doors and concealed exits, so the patient who's leaving never sees the one that's waiting.

"Here you sit and listen, and occasionally spin out one of your involved creations. And what major strides do you make for the greater mental health of the world? I'll tell you what.

In the course of about three years you slightly rearrange the neurotic ingredients in the lives of a total of about ten wealthy and self-centered people. That's your contribution to mankind, and for this you probably make about forty thousand dollars a year, and so far as I can tell nothing short of an atomic bomb can unseat you. Well, by God, I hope one falls.

"Your only stock in trade is a sort of crafty shrewdness, a tendency to suspect something rotten behind every decent thought and feeling. And such is the nature of this bloody world that I guess you're more often right than wrong. Well, you can have it. I'll have none of it. I've encountered more humanity in my garbage man than in you. And I happen to believe it's possible for people to have good thoughts and generous feelings that are not a cover for something mean and selfish. And I believe there are millions of people—and unanalyzed, mind you—who are more significantly furthering the common work of mankind than you.

". . . Sure it's childish. I know it's childish, but I don't care. I'd rather be a child like me than a grown-up like you. And one of these days, by God, I'll get free of you."

And so it comes about that he—he who, of all people, is most inept at voicing his own anger—becomes the target of hatred. He tosses in bed, he knows the night as well as day, he makes appointments till ten in the evening, his synapses click faster, his coronaries constrict, and in a small cramped hand he scratches out theories on the scroll of psychoanalytic time— but he can't keep up. He tries harder, he spins out more papers, he sees a far-away look in the eyes of his wife, the faces of his children become strange to him, but he can't keep up. He seldom sees the light of day, he immures himself in a million tons of masonry, behind a couch, and there he is trapped—caught between the forces, in himself and others, that he tried so deviously to manipulate: the isolate life he brings to his work, and the hatred and despair brought to him by those who suffer.

It seems, however, that he is also loved.

"I have a strange feeling, like being suspended in an unreal state . . . a vague unrest . . . waiting for something infinitely tragic and infinitely lovely. A feeling of sadness . . . . And yet there's joy in it, too—but a far-away benedictory joy, like at the end of a symphony. When I look at people I see good will and fondness. Not special people, anyone—a sales girl, a grocery clerk, anyone. They seem more human, more kind. Even when someone snarls at me I see some part of myself in his anger and know we are kin. The endless indignities of life don't goad me the way they used to. But the main feeling is one of sadness. I look at things as if I were seeing them for the last time. Lord knows I'm no Camille, yet I do this. I hear something of beauty and say, 'I will remember this,' as if I were here for only a short time.

". . . I know what all this means, but I'm afraid to tell you. I didn't know until yesterday, and then suddenly I knew. I remembered your saying that I had made 'much progress.' Not that I had forgotten it, but I realized yesterday that it had meant more to me than I knew, and perhaps more than you intended, because the feeling started the day you said that. It meant to me that maybe my analysis is nearly over. You've said nothing about ending it, but it's been two years now and I've felt much better recently. Maybe you didn't have this in mind. I don't know. But since then I've felt this dread. Because I don't want it to end—not now. I don't want it to end, and yet am ashamed to cling to you. I'm ashamed to be weak, now that I'm supposed to be strong, and I'm afraid I may be using time that someone sicker than I should have.

"But I know I'm not well yet. Since last week particularly I've felt such turmoil, uncertainty . . . . But I distrust even this. Maybe this, too, is a way of clinging. What is sickness? What is wellness? I don't know. I'm confused about every-thing. Is my analysis finished—and, if so, what's so conclusive about it now? Why not a month ago, or why not six months hence? . . . I don't know. I know only that if it's possible to rationalize keeping on, I'll find a way. And now I'm terrified by what I've said, since it might mean the analysis *should* end now.

"I'm ashamed of holding on to you . . . but I know why, and it doesn't seem strange. I'm ashamed only because it may disappoint you. No one has ever understood me and accepted me as you have. I know you like me. Don't, please, tell me this is transference. It's not. Everything you've done and said has indicated your understanding, and your willingness to accept me as a decent human being. No one else has done so much. I know now that it is I who have driven people away with hate. And now, perhaps, I can make some close relationships and not be so torn by fear and distrust that I destroy them. But still I'm not sure. Maybe I haven't changed at all. With you, though, I do feel sure. You know the worst and still accept me. Even when I've insulted you . . . .

"Oh God. . . . I'm thinking now of the things I've said in the past. The mean things . . . that tirade the day the old man fell in the street . . . the cheap accusations . . . day after day. And you never threw me out. Actually, as I now know, I was trying to make you throw me out. I fought you so hard because I could not believe your kindness was real. I had to believe it was fake. I had to bring it about that you would reject me. And then I would have used that rejection as one more proof that it's not safe to trust anyone.

"All that seems so long ago. I don't think I'll ever hate you again—though I've said that before, and been wrong. But everything seems different now. Recently I've found myself thinking more and more of you. It's hard to tell you. Whenever I see a blue car pass by, it's as though a magic wand were passed over my heart. It may be you. Or again, and this has happened, it may be your wife. When it's you I don't know whether to wave, or turn away and pretend I haven't noticed. And I have fantasies, a million fantasies, of being in your house, of playing with your children . . . our children . . . . How awful to need so much of one who needs nothing of me!"

Lean hands within him reach out hungrily. He longs to touch, to feel, to warm himself by this bright fire, so close, so near to hand, so unutterably far away. One slight movement and he could touch her hair. But he has so designed his life that it is as though there were a continent between them.

In these ways the problem of intimacy may be aggravated by the life-work that was meant to solve it, and on this problem some analysts founder. They withdraw from hatred, insulate themselves from their patients, and thereby preclude a therapeutic interaction. Or they yield to what appears as love and enter upon a personal relationship with a patient, a development which not only precludes therapy but also violates the moral commitment of an analyst.

But in view of the frequency with which the problem of intimacy determines the vocational choice, it is far more remarkable how few analysts founder in these ways. The majority survive the professional aggravation of their personal conflict. They come to seek other ways of dealing with the problem of intimacy, no longer expecting their work to provide a solution. They hang on, they persist, and eventually many of them prevail. They come to know with their hearts what they have always known with their heads—that the love and the hate are not for them, that transference is a reality. Living out their years in a climate of hatred and dependence and torment, they nevertheless maintain that the life of man has meaning, can be understood, and that his suffering is in part remediable. Though perhaps always slightly out of reach for themselves, they believe love and closeness to be achievable. They hold no brief for the greatness of their hearts—they are among the least of those who work beyond themselves—but to some extent they lessen the man-made misery of man. They stand by. Hatred they endure, and do not turn away. Love comes their way, and they are not seduced. They are the listeners, but they listen with unwavering intent, and their silence is not cold.

{ NOTES

Chapter I

[1] David Riesman, Nathan Glazer, and Revel Denny, *The Lonely Crowd* (New Haven: Yale University Press, 1950); Henry Steele Commager, *The American Mind* (New Haven: Yale University Press, 1950); Erik Erikson, *Childhood and Society* (New York: W. W. Norton & Company, 1950); Margaret Meade, *Male and Female* (New York: William Morrow & Company, 1949); Walter Lippman, *The Public Philosophy* (Boston: Little Brown & Company, 1955).

[2] The concept of social character refers not to the character of society, but, somewhat paradoxically, to the character of individuals. It is that nucleus of individual character which is shared by a significantly large social group. Since it is what we have in common with others, we take it for granted and most of the time are unaware of its existence.

[3] "Identity" is used throughout this work in its ordinary lay meaning. In psychoanalytic literature it bears a larger and more precise meaning, indicating a psychic organization which develops in successive phases throughout life, and which is partly unconscious. *Cf.* Erik Erikson, "The Problem of Ego Identity," *Journal of the American Psychoanalytic Association*, vol. 4, no. 1 (January, 1956), pp. 56–121.

[4] Quoted by Daniel Bell, "The Theory of Mass Society," *Commentary*, vol. 22, no. 1 (July, 1956), pp. 75–83.

[5] "Historical-mindedness is so much a preconception of modern thought that we can identify a particular thing only by pointing to the various things it successively was before it became that particular thing that it will presently cease to be." Carl L. Becker, *The Heavenly City of the Eighteenth-Century Philosophers* (New Haven: Yale University Press, 1932), p. 19.

[6] ". . . the patient of today suffers most under the problem of what he should believe in and who he should—or, indeed, might—be or become; while the patient of early psychoanalysis suffered most under inhibitions which prevented him from being what and who he thought he knew he was." Erik Erikson, *Childhood and Society* (New York: W. W. Norton & Company, 1950), p. 239.

[7] Norman Reider, "The Concept of Normality," *Psychoanalytic Quarterly*, vol. 19 (1950), pp. 43–51.

[8] ". . . we measure ourselves by many standards. Our strength and our intelligence, our wealth and even our good luck, are things which warm our heart and make us feel ourselves a match for life. But deeper than all such things, and able to suffice unto itself without them, is the sense of the amount of effort which we can put forth . . . . He who can make none is but a shadow; he who can make much is a hero." William James, *Psychology* (New York: Henry Holt & Company, 1892), p. 458.

Chapter II

[1] Psychoanalysis is both a comprehensive psychological theory and a theory and technique of treatment. These two are closely related, but are by no means the same. In this work, except where otherwise stated, the term refers only to the theory and technique of psychoanalytic therapy.

[2] This issue is taken up in detail in Chapter IV.

Chapter III

[1] Erich Fromm, "Individual and Social Origins of Neurosis," *American Sociological Review*, vol. 9 (1944), p. 380; reprinted in *Personality in Nature, Society and Culture*, edited by Clyde Kluckhohn and Henry Murray (New York: Alfred A. Knopf, 1948).

[2] Hans Meyerhoff, "Freud and the Ambiguity of Culture," *Partisan Review*, vol. 24, no. 1 (1957), p. 119.

[3] C. E. Ayres, *The Theory of Economic Progress* (Chapel Hill: The University of North Carolina Press, 1944), p. 101.

[4] *Ibid.*, Chap. VII.

[5] *Ibid.*, p. 137.

Chapter IV

[1] David Riesman, *Faces in the Crowd* (New Haven: Yale University Press, 1952), p. 23.

[2] Eric Hoffer, *The True Believer* (New York: Harper and Brothers, 1951).

[3] Daniel Bell, *op. cit.*, p. 82.

[4] "Right is what the right people do publicly, and vice versa." C. E. Ayres, *op. cit.*, p. 215. If private and public actions are at variance, morality is hypocritical. In matters of money and sex, as Freud has remarked, such hypocrisy is the rule in western civilization.

[5] "The repressive organization of the instincts seems to be *collective*, and the ego seems to be prematurely socialized by a whole system of extra-familial agents and agencies." Herbert Marcuse, *Eros and Civilization* (Boston: The Beacon Press, 1955), p. 97.

[6] David Riesman, Nathan Glazer, and Revel Denney, *op. cit.*, Chap. II.

[7] Abraham Edel, "Revolt Against Reason," *The Nation*, vol. 181, no. 22 (Nov. 26, 1955), p. 459.

[8] Carl L. Becker, *op. cit.*, p. 51.

Chapter V

[1] Barbara Wootton, quoted in *Time*, June 11, 1956, p. 50.
[2] C. E. Ayres, *op. cit.*, p. 93 ff.

Chapter VI

[1] Quoted by John Dewey, *Value, A Cooperative Inquiry*, edited by Ray Lepley (New York: Columbia University Press, 1949), p. 10.
[2] "Man who lives in a world of hazards is compelled to seek for security. He has sought to attain it in two ways. One of them began with an attempt to propitiate the powers which environ him and determine his destiny. It expressed itself in supplication, sacrifice, ceremonial rite and magical cult. In time these crude methods were largely displaced. The sacrifice of a contrite heart was esteemed more pleasing than that of bulls and oxen . . . ." John Dewey, *The Quest for Certainty* (New York: Minton, Balch and Company, 1929), p. 1.
[3] "It was . . . the perils of civil disobedience, not those of nature, which men sought to overcome by magic rite and mystic ecstasy . . . . In all probability horrendous rites go as far back in human experience as any tools; and as far back as intelligence and speech extend, doubtless men were trying to get the better of each other by hook or crook and most especially by hocus-pocus. Life has always held two sorts of perils for the sons of Adam: those implicit in the forces of nature, and those implicit in the coercions of social power systems." C. E. Ayres, in *Value, A Cooperative Inquiry, op. cit.*, p. 50.
[4] Emile Durkheim, *The Elementary Forms of the Religious Life* (London: George Allen and Unwin, Ltd., 1915), p. 419.
[5] Albert Camus, *The Myth of Sisyphus and Other Essays* (New York: Alfred A. Knopf, 1955).